Think Smart,
Move Fast

To Paul,

A imaginative conjective on the hist. of hi-tech, technology under capitalism, thoughtful contribution to the current debate on industrial, and foreign trade policies

Love

many, many more christmas a take care

Pops!

Greenville, Tex. 75401
12.12.84.

THINK SMART, MOVE FAST

Originally published as
The Super Executive's Guide to Getting Things Done

CHARLES H. FORD

 AMERICAN MANAGEMENT ASSOCIATIONS

This book is available at a special
discount when ordered in bulk quantities.
For information, contact Special Sales Department,
American Management Associations, Publications Group,
135 West 50th Street, New York, NY 10020.

Library of Congress Cataloging in Publication Data

Ford, Charles H., 1924–
  Think smart, move fast.

  Originally published: The super executive's guide to
getting things done. New York : American Management
Associations, c1982.
  Includes index.
  1. Management. I. Title.
HD31.F5725 1984   658   84–12328
ISBN 0-8144-7624-4

Printing Number

10 9 8 7 6 5 4 3 2 1

PREFACE to the PREFACE

Except for my cousin Albert, nothing is duller than a preface. I must confess to having seldom gotten beyond the first paragraph of one.

I've always felt that if the author really has something to say, he'll say it in the body of the book and that the preface serves only to tell you that he worked hard, did a whole lot of research, is well qualified to write whatever he's writing about, and wants to thank a whole host of people "who aided and assisted in this work and gave me encouragement to carry on when the going got rough, and without whose help and understanding this book could not have been written."

Ho hum.

Yet despite this unremitting antipathy, I will ask you to read *my* preface because:

1. I wrote it and think it's a great preface, and
2. It will establish the perspective from which this book should be read. And whatever value the book has will be enhanced because we both will be starting from the same contextual takeoff point.

So, read on.

PREFACE

Let's assume you come up with an idea for a great new product. You clean out your garage and spend your mornings making it. Afternoons you scurry about selling it. Suddenly you find that it has to be delivered and you've run out of time. So you hire a fellow to deliver it, and you spend your time selling and assembling. Business booms, and you need more time to sell and service your customers and administer the growing details of the business, so you hire someone else to put the product together.

Suddenly you come to realize not only that you have an organization but that you *depend* on this organization. If the guy putting the product together lets you down, you have nothing to sell. If your deliveryman lets you down, nothing gets delivered.

And with this comes the added sobering realization that all your creativity, all your efforts, mean precious little without the backing and support of this organization. It occurs to you that working alone means you are *limited* to the product of your own efforts, whereas working with an efficient organization can multiply these efforts or, conversely, working with an inefficient one can diminish them.

Most of us, of course, are involved with much larger, more complex, and more sophisticated organizations than the one just described, and this size, complexity, and sophistication often obscure the fact that we're no less dependent on this organization to multiply our efforts than if we were back to one assembler and one deliveryman.

How then to achieve this multiplication of effort and make these organizations and ourselves more effective? What this book will do is to zero in on three basic factors which have been generally ignored (incredibly!) and yet which lie at the very heart of organizational and individual effectiveness. I'll deal with these previously ignored concepts in a way that you'll find pretty universally applicable to any organization regardless of size or type.

Now ordinarily, we look askance at anyone who promises to deliver "universally applicable concepts." Such concepts are pretty risky rascals, somewhat like the perspective of the statistician who has his feet in a freezer and his head in an oven and says, "On the average, I feel pretty good." The point is, of course, that no two organizations are alike. Each develops its own personality and character; its own philosophy, work habits, and patterns; its own frames of reference with respect to the world around it. Each has its own unique leadership and its own unique response to that leadership. And each has its own unique levels of success or failure.

An organization is seldom, if ever, simply a mathematical sum of its individual inputs. More likely it will either equal *less*, if the inputs partially or wholly cancel each other out, or equal *more*, if they mesh and reinforce each other. The creation of this latter environment is our target.

If you take a pile of dynamite powder, spread it on an open field, and touch it off, it will go poof. But take the same powder, shape it, compact it, organize its individual granules into a cohesive mutually supportive entity, and touch it off (at this point, you'd better run like hell)—it will go BOOM!

Unfortunately, too many of our organizations go poof when they should go BOOM!

So, to help create the BOOM! we'll cover three main "universally applicable" subjects that are basic to getting the most out of both organizations and individuals, starting, perhaps, with ourselves.

We'll review the "super executive"—how he thinks and how

he approaches problem and opportunity situations. Inherent in and essential to the success of any organization is, of course, its leadership. We can obviously become better executives and better managers by understanding how these unique people, the super executives, function. We can learn from them—and they have a lot to teach us—if we can translate their approaches into easily understandable and adaptable terms. And I think I have.

We'll cover the "tempo climate" of an organization—that basic environment that governs how fast the organization gets things done, solves problems, and latches onto new opportunities. Once we understand what this is all about, we can measure our tempo, and the techniques for speeding it up become less difficult than one would expect.

Finally, we'll cover positive and negative thinking as it relates to new ideas. New ideas are obviously the spawning ground of organizational growth. If we're not ready for them when they come along or not disposed to find them when they don't, we've got trouble. Hopefully, I've put this into a perspective where one doesn't have to be a graduate psychologist to understand why new ideas either are aborted early on or are nurtured and developed instead.

One point of reassurance: None of what follows was written from the pristine isolation of an ivory tower. It was written from real-world observations, perceptions, and experiences— all filtered through, I think, a pretty coldly cynical eye. First of all, I'm a businessman who's on the firing line every day, fighting the battle of the plant and the marketplace. I pay for the mistakes my organization makes, and I rub my hands and chortle over our triumphs. I've put many of my observations into over 30 articles on organizational behavior, and I've had good feedback indicating I was hitting some pretty sensitive targets. Further, as a consultant, because of the intensity with which I protect confidences, I've had many doors opened for me through which has poured a whale of a lot of useful, solid information and insights not always available to others. Many of these insights are between the covers of this book.

With that in mind, let's get on to the super executive and see what that rascal has been up to while you've been spending time reading prefaces.

Charles H. Ford

CONTENTS

PART ONE

THE KEY TO THINKING SMARTER

CHAPTER 1

The Super Executive— His *Is* a Better Way!

My company molds expandable polystyrene (EPS), a plastic foam normally molded in soft low densities, used mostly for cushioned packaging. Several years ago, an injection molder of urethane plastics, a friend not noted for an overabundance of patience, phoned.

"Hello," I said pleasantly. "Never mind the hello," he snarled. "Right now most women's shoe heel wedges are made out of either wood or urethane. I mold them out of urethane. *I've* decided they should be made out of EPS because EPS *has* to be cheaper. We'll have to lick the problem of making them out of high-density EPS. *You'll* handle that! We'll make it a joint venture. You make; I'll sell. If you want the deal, be in my office tomorrow at 9 A.M." Pause. Click! Dial tone. "Good-bye," I said amiably.

Just before the call, I learned, he had been fingering one of his urethane heel wedges, a wedge that had been subject to considerable competitive price pressure. "There's got to be a better way than chasing price," he muttered. "I'm tired of matching pennies. There's an answer somewhere in using a different, less expensive material."

He thought for a moment, looked at the EPS (Styrofoam) disposable coffee cup from which he'd been drinking, looked back at the urethane wedge, then back to the coffee cup.

"Hell, that's it!" he said and reached for the phone.

The time it took him to lay the groundwork for his new industry: approximately three minutes, including the phone call.

Shake hands with a super executive.

Executives fall into three categories. At one extreme is the guy
who can take a seemingly simple situation and screw it up like
Hogan's goat by rendering it complex and zeroing in on the
wrong problems. He looks for answers peripheral to the core
issues and then takes forever and six minutes to make a decision—if he makes a decision at all.

At the other extreme is the executive who can take a seemingly complex situation, render it simple by quickly reducing
it to its essentials, and then go straight to what seems an obvious course of action. This, for want of a better name, is the
"super executive."

The third category is where most of us live, rattling around
somewhere between the two extremes.

The super executive is the guy who, coming upon a foun-
dering situation where others are pushing panic puttons and
charging off in a dozen different directions, calmly and instantly makes a rapid assessment of the situation, then takes
charge because he knows what to do next.

In organizations where he exists, he is the one to whom others instinctively turn for confirmation of their own judgments.
Out of the churning corporate cauldron, he generally surfaces
as *the* decision maker because he makes decisions with such
apparent ease and expresses them so positively and effortlessly
and with such confidence that others, less sure of themselves,
hesitate to quarrel with him. (Although as a matter of practi-
cality, he tends sometimes to be aggressive and impatient,
maybe tinged with arrogance, and unless he's a top manager,
he often makes some of the more established types feel threatened. They may react by setting ambushes or by magnifying

his mistakes. When they can they skirt his involvement altogether. Say hello to corporate politics.)

Most of us, when we make an earnest effort to deal with a problem, generally analyze it by painstakingly piling and meshing one fact upon another, all the while trying to separate the important from the unimportant, fighting the tendency to get sidetracked by the irrelevant and tangential, and priding ourselves on our calm, reasoned, logical approach and our ability to amass pertinent data. But that's *not* the way most super executives operate.

They have a "crux-sensitivity" in which their mental radars seem to take a problem or opportunity situation, cut right through the peripheral to lock in on the important and relevant, developing a feel for the core issues. They tend to interpolate rapidly. Given a few facts, they can generally fill in the gaps quickly. They can usually take in the totality of a situation (without getting sidetracked by its segments), quickly form generally accurate impressions, and from these impressions often make very rapid interpretative judgments. Unlike most of us, they *trust* these judgments. ("I feel it in my gut," said one super executive when questioned about the basis for several of his decisions, inviting no further conversation on the subject. Another dismissed the question, "Why hell, any damn fool can see it," with no explanation as to why "any damn fool can see it.") Consequently, they make fast decisions, so fast we frequently describe them as "intuitive" or "instinctive." ("Hip-shooting" is another description, one we sometimes mutter with lofty contempt when the super executive makes a decision in jig time that we've been working on for months, or when he attacks with remarkably clear logic one of our pet projects.)

If a super executive existed in pure form—which, of course, he doesn't—then this is how he would function. Obviously, super executive traits vary in both content and intensity. What he *isn't* is a caped figure with a big SE emblazoned on his chest. He is not faster than a speeding bullet, and if he tried to stop a moving freight train, he'd get knocked on his butt just as we would. But he does have certain qualities that set him apart as a decision maker, and if we come to understand them, we can learn from them. And if we do learn, then chances are we can give our business—or our jobs—a whole lot better, firmer, and more creative direction.

Over a period of several years I observed six executives I considered to be super executives. I was able to confirm my observations in discussions with their associates, subordinates, and others who were familiar with their behavior.

I had another thing going for me. In many instances, I could take a problem one of the executives dealt with and present the facts to several of the others for their assessments of the course of action they would take on the same problem. Almost as often, I could present the same issues to groups of non super executives (in the same companies) to see how they would approach them. As a result, a meaningful pattern emerged.

We've seen *what* the super executive does. Now let's look at some of the keys that unlock the process—in short, *how* they do it.

THE FIRST KEY

This first key is the master key to the whole process. Most of us when faced with a problem situation just naturally tend to focus our evaluation on the problem itself. Not so our super executives, who view the problem as merely a stepping stone to the *problem impact*—the effect of the problem. This becomes the focus of their evaluation, the takeoff point in the train of thought leading to a decision.

This is not a matter of playing cleverly with semantics or subtleties. The distinction is real—and critical—because these two different takeoff points generally lead to entirely different sequences of thought. Focusing on the problem impact tends to strip away the unimportant and peripheral in the evaluative process, and as we'll see in the following cases, it's also why the super executive can go to the core of a situation so quickly.

Case 1

A division of a miniconglomerate had a sewn-garment plant located in a sparsely populated rural area. Unfortunately, it soon found that it would have to compete for labor with a newly arrived machine tool plant whose high hourly rates served as a labor magnet. As a result, the garment plant's labor quality went from fair and placid to poor and restless. In its highly labor-intensive industry, it simply couldn't afford to raise its piecework rates enough to compete with the machine tool plant for available labor without pricing its products out of the marketplace.

In an all-day meeting to solve the problem, the corporate personnel director, plant manager, and group VP came up with some new inexpensive incentive programs, a few window-dressing fringe benefits, and an idea for publishing a monthly two-page mimeographed plant newspaper. "That'll goose up their morale," suggested the personnel director. "They'll feel like part of the family."

The president didn't think so. "This is a classic case of dead-horse whipping," he grumbled when presented with the results of their deliberations. "This will solve nothing except maybe prolong the agony for another month or two. The simple fact is that we just can't compete with the tool company for what little labor there is and all these Mickey Mouse gyrations won't change *that* fact." His decision: "We'll relocate the plant to a labor surplus area." His time input: about 12 minutes.

While his subordinates took the problem and said, "O.K.,

we've got a labor problem situation to deal with here," the
president took the same situation and said, "Our labor problem has screwed up our ability to produce competitively
(problem impact), therefore we've got a plant location situation
to deal with."

   That the president's approach to a problem situation is typical of most super executives was confirmed when I presented
this case to five other super executives and five non super executives. Exhibit 1 illustrates the pattern of their responses.

EXHIBIT 1. Super executive and non super executive approaches to
Problem 1.

Breakdown of the Problem-Situation	Pattern of Thinking	
	5 out of 6 Non Super Executives*	4 out of 6 Super Executives*
The problem?	**Poor labor quality and labor unrest** (*focus*)	Poor labor quality and labor unrest
The problem impact (*the effect of the problem*)?		**Our inability to produce competitively** (*focus*)
The cause of the problem?	Our inability to meet competitive wages	
The cause of the problem impact?		Location of the plant in a tight labor market
What to do about it?	Develop new inexpensive incentive programs, window-dressing fringe benefits, etc. (*attacking the cause of the problem*)	Move the plant to a labor surplus area (*attacking the cause of the problem impact*)

*Including the case company's executives.

Case 2

A custom packaging manufacturing company faced a sharp, sudden upturn in sales. It couldn't have come at a worse time. In six weeks it was scheduled to shut down for vacation, during which time essential equipment maintanance had to be done. Its joint sales–production team decided to go on overtime for the six-week period and build up its inventory to carry it over the shutdown period. Three weeks later, the head shipper called a meeting. "You're going to have to back off, fellas. My warehouse is bursting. I have no more room."

Acknowledging the need to ease the warehouse problem, the group considered several alternatives, including asking customers to accept goods before scheduled shipping dates. "No good," said the VP of sales. "Most of them have less room than we have." How about offering extra dating or temporary price reductions as added incentives? "No good," said the VP. "In these times, you give these people dating or a lower price even on a temporary basis and you'll sweat bullets trying to get them back where they belong after the crunch. They'll look at it as a price increase."

"O.K.," they concluded. "Then let's cut back production by going back on straight time and maybe shutting down a press or two. By being cleverly selective, we'll try to minimize the hoopla when we don't ship some customers on time."

To determine which jobs to slough off on, accounts were analyzed and estimates made of what they thought were their customers' real needs. Two and a quarter hours into this complex, ramification-fraught rescheduling, the president walked in and was introduced to the problem. "We're going to have to balance our production with our warehouse capacity," he was told. "This means cutting back on production until after vacation."

The president shook his head. "Hell, you can't jeopardize sales because our warehouse is full. The problem isn't too much production, it's too little space!" Turning to the head shipper, he directed, "Get on the phone, rent some trailers, park them in the yard, and load them with what you can't stuff into the warehouse. It's going to mean double handling for a while, but that's a hell of a lot better than losing sales, antagonizing customers, and having our reputation for on-time delivery jeopardized." His time input: a little less than two minutes.

This case was presented to five other super executives and four non super executives for the course of action they would take. The results are shown in Exhibit 2.

As both these cases illustrate—and here's the core of the first key—the initial focal (or takeoff) point generally determines

EXHIBIT 2. Super executive and non super executive approaches to Problem 2.

Breakdown of the Problem-Situation	Pattern of Thinking	
	3 out of 5 Non Super Executives*	4 out of 6 Super Executives*
The problem?	**Overcrowded warehouse** (*focus*)	Overcrowded warehouse
The problem impact (*the effect of the problem*)?		**Potential loss of sales because of inadequate inventory** (*focus*)
The cause of the problem?	Too much production buildup for warehouse capacity	
The cause of the problem impact?		Lack of warehouse space
What to do about it?	Cut back production (*attacking the cause of the problem*)	Increase warehouse space (*attacking the cause of the problem impact*)

*Including the case company's executives.

the train of thought that follows. The super executive starts perking with the problem impact, then goes in a straight line from this to the cause of the problem impact and then to the correction of that cause. (Chances are when someone says with admiration, "Old Herman has that knack of quickly reducing a complex situation to its simplest essentials," Old Herman is doing nothing more than defining the problem in terms of its problem impact.)

Starting from the problem instead of the problem impact invariably results in a narrower evaluation of the total situation, and final decisions are less prone to be fully responsive to overall needs. Because seeking but not finding a solution that is truly responsive often leads to a feeling of incompleteness, the time input of those focusing on the problem, as they grope with a limited range of alternatives, is often considerably longer and invariably less productive than the time input of those focusing on the problem impact.

THE SECOND KEY

The second key deals with two principles: "precedent-constraint" and "constant-constraint." Precedent-constraint is what generally results when we evaluate problem situations in terms of those familiar solutions with which we have in the past attacked seemingly similar situations. Constant-constraint is what generally results when we evaluate a problem that has certain elements that appear to be and are accepted as constants. Both types of constraints set up unconscious barriers to our thinking.

In the garment plant case, for example, the executives had had considerable experience in personnel management and their natural inclination was to solve what they saw as a labor problem in terms of their past experiences in dealing with other labor problems. This locked their thinking into a conventional labor–management approach. At the same time, without giving it conscious thought, they simply accepted the location of the plant as the constant, the fixed element in the situation around which they had to work.

In the packaging company case, the executives had had a great deal of experience in juggling machine schedules. They did it all the time for a variety of reasons. In addition, they considered the finite dimensions of the warehouse as the constant they had to deal with. It just never occurred to them that they could change these dimensions. Influenced by these two constraints, they saw the problem as a simple scheduling one and limited their thinking to that.

Score a big plus for starting with the problem impact as the focal point—starting from there, neither president was bound by these constraints. Since they did not focus on the problems, they were not subject to the precedent-constraints associated with solving seemingly similar past problems. And they were not bound by constant-constraints, because a problem-impact approach generally sees all elements as flexible, subject to change, reversal, or correction.

THE THIRD KEY

The third key relates to the perspective from which a person looks at his job and role in the organization. Normally, we assume that an executive is by definition basically concerned with the contribution of his efforts to translating asset use into profits and that therefore every manager looks at his job in that light. T'aint so. When a non super executive, especially in middle and lower levels of management, is asked to define his job, he tends to do so in terms of his functional responsibilities ("functional awareness"). The super executive, on the other hand, tends to answer in terms of his contribution to profits ("profit awareness"). (On a practical basis, the higher an executive goes, the closer he gets to ultimate profit responsibility, and the more his profit awareness is sharpened. This applies to both super and non super executives.) While this attitudinal difference may seem picayune, the fact is there is a very real, albeit subtle, fine line between the two awarenesses that produces different results.

To catch both super and non super executives off guard, I threw the question out in the middle of discussions dealing with entirely different matters. Asking for a quick one-sentence definition of their jobs, I got the following replies, which are both typical and illustrative of the two awarenesses.

"My job is to put everything together so we make money," said one super executive. Said another, "I've got plenty of competent people who can take in raw materials at one end of the plant and turn out finished goods at the other. My job is to see to it that they do it the best way at the least cost." A super executive VP of marketing said, "I can sum it up in a few words. My job is to sell more than last year and make a good buck on everything I sell."

In contrast, non super executives gave such answers as "My job is to run this company." "I'm in charge of plant operation." "My job is to develop and market our product line."

This simple, basic attitudinal difference ties in with the first two keys when we consider that problem impacts tend to have a *cost or profit base*, whereas problems tend to have a *functional base*. The conclusion seems to be inescapable that if a person thinks of his job in terms of his contribution to the ultimate corporate goal of making money as opposed to his functional responsibilities, he is more apt to be sensitive to problem impacts and less apt to be influenced by the constraints of "precedents" and "constants."

THE FOURTH KEY

Opportunity situations are those in which a potential advantage can be gained from doing something new or different. They obviously start with new ideas. Saying that a common

thread among super executives is that they are positive think-
ers when it comes to new ideas seems rather obvious. We'll
pretty much leave it at that for now because the whole area of
positive and negative thinking will be closely examined in Part
Three of this book.

For the moment, let's accept the fact that negatively oriented
executives tend to perceive new ideas primarily in terms of the
problems of implementation and the potential risks. This is
their starting point. Positively oriented executives perceive new
ideas initially in terms of their profit potential (the "opportunity impact"). Like problem versus problem impact or profit
awareness versus functional awareness, this distinction also
leads to two different takeoff points, which lead in turn to two
different trains of thought and thus generally to two different
conclusions. Focusing first on the problems of implementation
and potential risks of new ideas often tends to be *destructive*
to potential opportunity. Whereas focusing first on the profit
potential of new ideas tends to be *constructive*.

Our friend the urethane molder is a good example of this
principle in action. He saw the use of EPS in women's heel
wedges as a unique money-making idea. The technical problems of molding high-density EPS were secondary. He sensed
that somehow when the time came they could be solved and
the profit potential of the idea would provide the necessary
incentive. The idea got rolling and translated into a profit opportunity because he refused to let his thinking or his enthusiasm get hung up at the initial stages by the problems of implementation. A non super executive might well have thought
of the idea, considered first the magnitude of the problems,
and said, "Let's forget it. It's too risky. It's never been done
before."

Starting the evaluation of a new idea by concentrating initially on its profit potential is what gives most super executives' thinking that forward thrust that enables them to better
control future events rather than simply react to them. Again,

the attitudinal differences may appear subtle, but the results are anything but.

THE FIFTH KEY

The fifth key is the element of time. When most of us are presented with a problem, we often break it down into components we feel we can best work with. We amass some data, evaluate it, probably discuss it at length with others. We sort out alternatives until we reach one that satisfies us. Often we'll put the problem aside in the middle of the process and come back to it later. All this takes time, which potentially leaves plenty of room for tangential flights, misanalyses, and possibly loss of touch with the core issues. (Admittedly, for some non super executives, it also leaves time for thoughtful input and creative idea germination—which goes to prove that nothing in life is all black or all white.)

On the other hand, our super executives in following their straight-line train of thought tend to use far less time to solve problems. The brevity of expression that comes out generally reflects the economy of thought that has gone in, and the tight time frame leaves little room and less encouragement for the peripheral and unimportant, and almost no room for the tangential.

While there is little question of a direct relationship between the two, it is not clear to what extent brevity of time input is a factor in developing "crux-sensitivities" and to what extent it is the product of it. And at this point, it's enough to say that, when a person is both able and prone to analyze a situation in a few cogent sentences, little time is available for the irrelevant and the conditioning effect is to think in core terms. All this ties in with the fact that problem impacts are about as "core-termish" as you can get.

Time is important to super executives. Patience is not one

of their strong points. Relegating a decision or a pending problem to the back burner is an irritant. "Let's think about it for a while" (when *they* have already given it enough thought) or "Let's sleep on it and talk about it tomorrow" often sets their teeth on edge. To save time, they are often willing to forgo information input. ("Don't bother taking the time to develop those figures now. We can make a pretty good guess at them—at least sufficient to pick up a direction.")

SUMMING UP THE FIVE KEYS

To sum up the five keys that unlock the super executive's approach to problem situations:

1. Super executives use the problem as a stepping stone to the problem impact (usually the cost or profit-based effect of the problem). From this takeoff point, their thinking goes straight to an identification of the cause of that problem impact, then to a solution that removes that cause.

2. Because a problem impact is a step beyond the problem itself, the super executive's thinking is not limited by precedent- or constant-constraints, both of which are usually associated with solving problems as opposed to problem impacts.

3. The super executive's job perspective involves a greater emphasis on cost and money making than on function.

4. In the same vein, super executives are positively oriented toward new ideas, starting their evaluation from the profit potential of the idea, not from the problems and risks involved in implementing it (which they get into later after they've built up a good head of enthusiastic steam). This tends to give them an acute sensitivity to new opportunities, with a resultant forward thrust to their thinking.

5. Finally, efficient use of time is important. This generally involves an economy of both thought input and expression output—which encourages a devotion to core issues.

It's apparent that all five keys bear some cause-and-effect relationship to one another. If you feel more comfortable changing the order of these relationships, be my guest.

For example, one might suggest that profit awareness leads to a breaking of the barriers of the two constraints, which in turn leads to a tendency to view situations in terms of their problem impacts. Or one might say that the time key leads to a tendency to view situations in terms of their problem impacts, which in turn breaks the barriers of the two constraints.

Whew! Pass the aspirin.

HOW SUPER EXECUTIVES APPROACH DECISIONS

In their approach to decisions, the most profound characteristic of our super executives is their propensity for making high-risk decisions. Obviously, some of this is built into their jobs. If the president, for example, decides to buy a $1 million piece of equipment, that represents a pretty high-risk decision but one probably well within his province. If on the other hand, a junior engineer makes the same decision and tries to implement it, he's apt to find himself pretty damn quick in the local unemployment line. Their jobs and their profit responsibilities call for different levels of decisions with different levels of risk.

But the difference goes beyond this to a different philosophy about what a decision should do. This can best be defined in terms of the difference between an incremental or palliative solution that nips at the problem and "solution totality" (a phrase from one of our super executives) in which the total problem is attacked so that in most cases after the solution has been applied, the problem is no longer recognizable (although the solution itself may create a whole new range of problems).

Incremental or palliative solutions generally take care of part of the problem or stall its effects. Taken in steps, they usually can be closely monitored and often easily reversed. There's very little risk and often not a whole lot of solution. Total solutions, on the other hand, involve wider actions, whose ultimate results are often less predictable and which by their very scope call for more investment or bridge burning.

My introduction to solution totality came many years ago and left a lasting impression. At the time, I was trying to sell a skeptical North Carolina truck parts jobber on becoming a distributor for a relatively unknown line of truck batteries. My charm and good nature persevered. A deal was struck.

One of the partners accompanied me to the combination counter–stockroom section to tell his people to prepare for a shipment of batteries. Decision time. Where to put them?

A plaster board partition ran away from the counter at 90°. A temporary one put up years ago, it had served its purpose and for no particular reason had simply been left in place. It created a narrow space between itself and the outer wall. The partner nudged me. "Watch this," he said. Five people discussed the problem for about 20 minutes. Finally, leaning toward putting the batteries behind the temporary partition, they recognized new problems. Every time they wanted a battery, they would have to walk the length of the partition to the open end and then walk back, and since the partition allowed little light in the area, they'd be walking in the dark. More discussion. Little progress. I had visions of passing two birthdays rooted to the spot before a firm decision was made.

Finally, the partner could take it no longer. "Son," he said, "I'm going to give you a lesson in management."

He ambled across the room to a position opposite the partition. His ambling was no easy matter, as his six-foot frame carried 355 pounds of muscle, bone, and fat. Turning, he lumbered toward the partition, gaining momentum like a 747 on takeoff. Belly first (he had little choice) he crashed into the partition, splintering it in 15 directions. Turning to his five people, he snarled, "There, that takes care of your problem, doesn't it?"

Returning to where I had watched in silent fascination, he said, "That's your lesson in management. You have a problem? Don't fool with it. Zap it!"

He had a point.

MORE REASONS FOR TAKING RISKS

This propensity for taking higher risks reflects the last segment of the train of thought that starts with the problem impact and ends with an attack on the elements causing the problem impact. This approach is generally more far reaching and thus more risky than merely seeking a problem solution.

A medium-size manufacturer of frozen food products depended on its ability to bring out a constant stream of new frozen foods. The usual path was from R&D to market testing to full-scale production and distribution. The time from release from R&D to full-scale marketing was approximately 10 or 11 months—a length of time that irritated the company's new president. Not only was this just plain too slow, but several times the competition picked up on the new products and swooped the market while his company was still mired in the market-testing stage.

"No good," said the president. "We've got to move faster. Of all the elements in the chain, market testing takes the longest." His subordinates agreed. "O.K.," they said. "We'll see what we can do to reduce the market-testing time." "You missed the point," retorted the president. "I don't want to reduce it. I want to *eliminate* it."

"Sure," said his subordinates. "We'll try it with one product and see what happens." "You still don't read me," said the president. "Not someday and no crutches. From here on, no more market testing, period. From here on, we're going to have to take our chances with our judgment as to what will or won't sell. If we're smart and know our market, we'll do just fine. If we don't know our market, we'll soon find out, and it'll be butt-kicking time in spring."

Exhibit 3 outlines the president's and the subordinates' different lines of thought, which led to different conclusions and different levels of risk.

An interesting footnote: The time gap dropped to approximately five or six months. To date, of six products brought out without testing, four have been successful. The results of an-

EXHIBIT 3. President's approach versus subordinates' approach to a problem.

Breakdown of the Problem-Situation	President's Line of Thinking	Subordinates' Line of Thinking
The problem?	Long time gap between R&D and full-scale production and distribution	**Long time gap between R&D and full-scale production and distribution** (*focus*)
The problem impact (*the effect of the problem*)?	**Loss of potential profit because of inability to bring more products on stream faster and to protect new products against competitive piracy** (*focus*)	
The cause of the problem?		The time it takes to market-test
The cause of the problem impact?	Market testing, the longest part of the time chain	
What to do about it?	Eliminate market testing, substitute executive judgments: total solution (*attacking the cause of the problem impact*)	Find ways to reduce market testing time: incremental solution (*attacking the cause of the problem*)

other are incomplete, but indications point to at least moderate success. One bombed. This compares with a 60–70 percent previous success rate. The group making the decision had a total of 82 years experience in the industry. This experience substituted for market testing. So far, so good.

Another reason super executives take higher risks is their compelling impatience. "If you peck away at a problem," said one of our super executives, "it'll probably change at the same rate as your partial solutions, so you end up spinning your wheels just to stay even. My feeling is, if you have a problem, do what has to be done to get rid of it once and for all. I don't have the temperament to deal with some variation of the same damn problem over and over again."

Because of their confidence in the quality of their judgments, most super executives don't see the same degree of risk in their decisions as others less sure of themselves might see. Thus, what appears to be a high-risk decision to some executives is often perceived by a super executive as involving less risk.

Finally, and by no means the least important reason for their propensity toward high-risk decisions, super executives tend to make more non-defense-oriented decisions. Many non super executives, especially those who are insecure in their jobs, tend to make decisions they hope can be defended later with sound data-supported arguments, so if the decision's results sour and they're called upon to explain how come, they've covered their butts. As a result, they often seek an inordinate amount of confirming data and support from others, and many times attempt to make decisions on a share-the-responsibility basis. This preoccupation with how well they can defend a decision later rather than with the *effect* of the decision itself has a tremendous influence on the nature of the decisions they make. (They tend to be incremental decisions, for example.) The super executive, on the other hand, tends to make more unilateral decisions with far less defense-oriented data. They are more prone, as noted, to defend a judgment with an impatient, "Why hell, any damn fool can see it." (Translation: "I can see it, and I know I'm right. If you can't, that's your problem.")

Many times a non super executive will exhibit this super executive trait until he comes right down to making the decision, at which point he will back off, suddenly fearful of the consequence of possible error. At this final decision point, he switches gears, often erring on the side of caution, or defers making the decision while casting about for a more defensible one. Unfortunately, most defense-oriented decisions are not often wholly responsive to the problem or opportunity they attempt to address.

SOME PERSONAL TRAITS

Before looking at some of the super executive's personal traits, a word of caution. Beware the counterfeit super executive. An executive may look like a super executive, sound like one, even smell like one, yet be the antithesis of a super executive.

Making snap decisions, running roughshod over the opposition, resorting to convoluted logic to "prove" a point, tossing off evaluations and pompous judgments like snowflakes in a blizzard doesn't make a super executive. Styles may blend and blur, but not substance. The counterfeit super executive is perhaps the victim of too many General Patton movies, or perhaps he has worked with a super executive, noted his style and success, and said to himself, "Aha! So that's how it's done!" although he himself would not be able to recognize a core issue if it fell on him.

The counterfeit super executive often tries to compensate for his deficiencies by acting arrogant. Rather than make a forward-thrusting, constructive, creative contribution to the organization, he tends to be a disruptive influence, often contributing little but confusion, dissension, and screwed-up decisions.

So much for this character.

Back to the super executive's personal traits.

Most super executives are pretty self-assured. Mix this with their tendency to be impatient and to function at a high speed and the result is a bent toward abruptness, lack of subtlety, and tactlessness. If we're on the receiving end, we're apt to mutter, "Arrogant bastard"—and sometimes we may be right. The fact is most everyone interprets his own actions as being "right," and often when a super executive perks along at a pretty good clip, he assumes anyone not perking at the same rate or not immediately responsive to his demands for translating his thinking into appropriate action is both obstructive and a loser. Such is life with a super executive . . . sometimes.

"Tough minded" is another description often applied to the super executive—a cliché, perhaps, but not one without merit. On a practical basis, it is the ability to make decisions, without agonizing over them, that may have the collateral result of inflicting pain on other people. Much of this results from the super executive's tendency to narrow his straight-line field of vision between problem impact and solution, thus eliminating the peripheral. Unfortunately, the fate of people who are adversely affected by many such decisions lies in the periphery. For example, super executives often fire subordinates easily. The fact that the subordinate is a human being with perhaps a mortgage to pay, a wife to feed, and three kids to educate is less important to them than the impersonal problem impact that the subordinate is not getting his job done. If they suggest closing a plant, which would result in an economic dislocation to the community, again it is probably because closing the plant represents a straight-line solution to a problem impact, with the adversely affected community on the periphery.

Happily, not all super executives I've observed fit this mold. Many times the human factor *does* temper their final decisions. The distinction is that they often amend their initial decisions *after* they are made but before they are implemented, to adjust for the human factor, rather than taking the human factor into account *first* and letting it influence their decisions. Thus, they tend to better understand the full scope of their trade-offs.

Despite this self-assurance, impatience, and tough-mindedness, most super executives respect opposition or conflict, but generally when it is on substantive issues and strongly asserted. "Tell me I'm wrong," said one typically. "If I am and you save me from making a mistake, you win points. But don't nitpick, and be damn sure it's what you really think. Don't fight me just for the sake of arguing or to show me how smart you are."

THE SUPER EXECUTIVE IN PERSPECTIVE

I don't want to give a false impression. It is not my thesis that all super executives are omniscient supermen cloaked in mantles of infallability, while all others are pretty much floundering dolts merely riding on the back of the super executive. In many cases, a super-executive-to-be functions at a low key in the organization, his budding super-executiveness hidden just below the visible horizon, simply because at this point in his career he lacks the authority to express or implement his judgments.

Obviously, many *apparent* non super executives are highly competent, thoughtful, thorough, and creative, and many of these rise to the top of the executive heap. But the point is, if you scratch one of these, chances are you'll find more super executive traits than may appear on the surface. It becomes more a matter of expression than of substance.

The super executive is not necessarily the best manager, especially when it comes to managing the activities of others. His ego, personal ambition, impatience, and often tactlessness can sometimes be a turnoff rather than an inspiration. He can confuse driving with leading.

When he's right, he can be very right. And, because of the magnitude of the decisions he tends to make, when he goofs, he can goof badly. Sometimes he's quick to correct his mistakes with the same total-solution approach that brought about the original decision. But not always. Some—and this obviously varies from super executive to super executive and from case to case—stick by their decisions, reluctant to accept that maybe their judgments were wrong and their subordinates or peers, and often bosses, were right after all. Often they will try to shift the blame to the implementers for screwing up their decisions.

And some of their decisions can go whacko. Identifying and assessing the scope of the problem impact is, in the final analysis, a judgmental evaluation. Like anyone else, super executives can be wrong. They can also be stubborn. And they can rely on their intuition to the extent of sometimes going off half-cocked with insufficient information. Their self-confidence, perhaps built on a long string of successes, can cross the line to arrogance, and pretty soon they may stop listening to opposing opinions. At this point, they can be less than useful, if not disruptive, to the organization.

But in the main, they do have a unique approach to problems and opportunities that many of us can learn from and adapt to our own managerial methodology, because whatever else can be said about super executives, by and large they are the doers and the movers. They are the guys who make it happen!

CHAPTER 2

Cranking Some Super Executive Methodology into the Organization

Three perspectives:

"The greatest of all wisdom is to know thyself," Socrates

"To first understand oneself is to then understand the world," Spengler

"One cannot know any other man save that one knows himself," Pliny the Elder

"Could be. But given the incentive, you can still learn one helluva lot from the super executive," C. H. Ford (a second perspective)

"Super executive, schuper executive. Eat your dinner," Ford's old grandmother (a third and not necessarily pertinent perspective)

My old grandmother's opinion notwithstanding, knowledge of how the super executive operates is important for three reasons:

1. If we are associated with one, it gives us a better understanding and appreciation of how and why he thinks as he does and how to use his talents. If we have a better feel for the source of his judgments, we can deal with those judgments more confidently and perhaps reduce the possibility of conflict because of differences in style.

2. It will give us a better standard against which to gauge our own mental processes and approaches. It can help us develop any latent super executive qualities that may be just below the surface waiting for that little bit of change in perspective to bring them bubbling up. Or, if we are lucky enough to have some of these qualities, it can give us a better understanding of what they are and can certainly help us sort them out and perhaps even sort out our relationships with others not so endowed.

3. Understanding those super executive qualities that are positive attributes can serve as a working tool for infusing them, to whatever extent possible, into the thinking patterns of our organizations.

With regard to this last point, the incentive for encouraging both a personal and organizational push in this direction should be pretty strong. It will come as no great revelation to anyone that every organization is constantly laced with operational problems and that new opportunities float by from time to time. To focus on these instead of on the problem impacts or opportunity impacts can misdirect the thrust of the organization and erode corporate momentum while energizing the institution of nit-picking. This not only eats up a whole lot of time better spent on other things but also can result in the constant repetition of the same or similar problems and the continual neglect of opportunities that keep floating right by us, untapped.

If we could learn only one thing from the super executive, it should be his problem-impact approach to decisions. This is the cornerstone of his super executiveness, and many of the other super executive qualities flow from it. The more this business of distilling problem impacts out of problem situations permeates an organization, the more it can become its common language and thinking pattern and the more effective that organization will be, unless it is hopelessly populated with nincompoops, in which case only nincompoopery will permeate. Like most other things, the degree of permeation, especially in the initial stages, is generally in direct proportion to the intensity of effort.

There is no great mystery to the process. It doesn't take an advanced degree in psychology or years of poring over learned tomes (a good thing, too, since there aren't any learned tomes on the subject). The difference between the super executive and the non super executive is not wholly a question of smarts, it's partially a question of perspectives, and the line between profit awareness and functional awareness or problems and problem impacts is not so great that it can't be crossed without a whole lot of effort.

APPLYING THE SUPER EXECUTIVE APPROACH TO THE ORGANIZATION

In the last chapter, we saw how the super executive approach works at higher levels. Let's see what happens when it seeps through to other levels.

In our industry, we get our raw material in the form of very fine spherically shaped crystals, or beads. Each tiny bead encapsulates a blowing agent that expands when exposed to heat and in turn expands the bead. This process of heat exposure under very tightly controlled conditions is called the "expansion process" (what else?). The amount of expansion determines the density in pounds per cubic foot of the bead to be used in the molding process. Sometimes the raw material manufacturer ships in a bad lot of bead, which lumps in the expansion process as one bead welds to another, and this fouls up the molding process downstream by clogging feeders.

For years when lumping occurred, our expansion man and plant manager would fiddle with the air and steam pressures, resident times, and other factors in the process, looking for the right combination that would enable them to delump the bead and make it suitable for plant use. This was a case of purposely doing something wrong so it would come out right. Only these two people in the plant had the ability, know-how, and experience to correct the problem once it occurred. They viewed the use of these talents as a unique part of their jobs. When they were successful, which was not always, their efforts were applauded.

The plant manager's perspective of his role in this was based on his functional awareness of his job. This was to keep the plant running, and that took expanded bead. No one, therefore, viewed his contribution as anything but a productive effort to do this job. His view of the lumping bead problem looked like this:

Problem: Lumping bead.
Cause of problem: A defective lot of raw material.
What to do about it? By educated trial and error, change normal expansion process procedures to compensate for and overcome raw material defects. Give it the old college try even though the results are not always wholly successful.

After being introduced to the problem-impact principle (O.K., maybe not "introduced." How about "hammered into"?), his approach swung around 180°. Asking first "What can we do to make the defective bead usable?" was seeking a problem solution. Instead he now sought to identify the cost/profit-based effect of the problem (the problem impact) and from this to find a problem-impact solution.

Once the plant manager became sensitive to it, distilling the problem impact out of the right cost/profit-based questions was not as difficult as it first seemed. The questions he now asks run something like this:

Question: "Where and what will it cost if we do nothing about the problem?"

Answer: "We'll lose production because of clogged feeders. Exactly how much I don't know and I don't care. I just know it's enough, so we damn well can't do nothing."

Question: "O.K., given the fact that we must do something, how are we now reacting and what is the cost of that reaction on a cost/profit producing area?"

Answer: "We're diddling with expansion process techniques that may or may not work. This has a cost in time and, since expanded bead has a short shelf life, it will probably cost in lost production. While we're playing around trying to make a defective lot of bead usable, we're not expanding the non-defective lots the plant needs to keep operating.

Now the new problem-impact approach frames up this way:

1. First, the problem: Lumping bead.
2. Then the problem impact: The lumping bead is costing in lost production and in time by tying up two men with a potential of iffy results.
3. The *cause* of this problem impact: Trying to make a bad lot of bead usable.
4. Finally, the evaluation and decision (the attack on the cause of the problem impact): Even if we succeed in making it work, it's going to cost money in time and probably some lost production dollars, so we'll fool around with it only long enough to establish that the bead is defective beyond *minor* expansion process corrections. We'll attack the cause of the problem impact by increasing our storage space and maintaining a higher level of emergency backup raw material inventory so we can simply return the defective bead to the manufacturer without taking a chance of running out of material.

Obvious? Maybe. But for seven years so was his first approach, which seemed so logical in a functional awareness environment that no one ever thought to question it.

Realistically, the problem-impact approach is not a panacea. It still requires judgmental decisions, because conclusions don't always flow in a smooth line once the problem impact has been identified. For instance, it's possible that the plant manager might have come to the conclusion that the costs of storage space and of maintaining a high enough backup inventory, the infrequency of the problem, and the wear and tear of returning a defective shipment would outweigh the cost in time and its possible effects on production, and he would opt for continuing his original approach. Or he might feel that the occasional defective shipment would not warrant muddying his relationship with his bead supplier. These are evaluative judgments. If he's smart, he'll make more right ones than wrong ones. If he's not, he'll be wrong more often and is likely to find himself on his butt out in left field. The point is, of course, a manager will seldom be able to make effective evaluations unless the problem is first put into a perspective that sets the stage for an assessment of cost/profit trade-offs.

DEEPER PERMEATIONS

As the problem-impact principle took a firmer set, the plant manager began to look at equipment downtime, not in terms of just a downed piece of equipment requiring repair (problem), but rather as lost production and shipments (problem impact). "Every hour a press is down is not just an hour gone by. It's $480 of lost production." He directed that from then on all weekly downtime reports be in terms of these lost production dollars "so we can all see what the hell it's really costing us."

He found that a report that states "Press #12, leaking booster pump. Fixed. $1,200 lost production" has far more relevancy and effect than one that states "Press #12, leaking booster pump. Fixed. Down 2½ hours." The job of keeping equipment running now took on a new perspective—and more importantly, a new sense of meaning and urgency on the part of his maintenance people. They adopted the attitude of "Let's do it quick and get it right the first time, because if these dollars of lost production show up again next week on the same press for the same reason, then it's obvious we're not doing our jobs, we're costing the company money, and old bull-of-the-woods plant manager is going to chew us out."

Although the fallout from the plant manager's new problem-impact profit/cost orientation went on and on, we'll follow the effect of permeation only one more step. For one month, he analyzed breakdowns that cost over $2,000 each in lost production and discovered that most were minor problems that had been prolonged because of a lack of on-hand spare parts. By simply instituting a new inventory procedure for spare parts, he reduced downtime by almost 23 percent. When the maintenance reports had been written in terms of sterile hours, the reaction was ho hum. After all, equipment downtime is a fact of factory life. But when it was listed in meat-and-potatoes lost production dollars (cost/profit-based problem impact), bells rang, sirens blew, the red action flag popped up, and the cost of maintaining a higher spare-parts inventory came across as piddling compared to what it saved.

ANOTHER EFFECT

Other super executive traits tend to flow from the problem-impact approach—its effect on precedent- and constant-constraints, for example.

As a substitute for an expensive process now commonly used in the steel casting business, a plastics molder was negotiating a contract to mold several thousand plastic parts for a steel foundry. This was a new approach, never before tried. A 45-pound core was to be shipped from the foundry, molded *into* the plastic part, and then shipped as one piece (plastic part and core) back to the foundry for casting.

In working out the details, it became apparent that handling the 45-pound core would create a serious problem. Delicate and easily broken, the core required special techniques for shipping, which had to be devised. The plastics plant used women press operators, and their ability to handle the heavy cores was seen as still another problem.

To solve these problems, two foundry executives met with two plastics company executives. All had engineering backgrounds. The plastics company's sales manager, *not* an engineer, also attended. In reviewing the problems, the engineers naturally inclined toward engineering solutions. Their thinking was locked into precedents ("This is how we solve materials handling problems") and constants ("The insertion of the core into the plastic during the molding process is a must. *How* we do it is what we're here for."). After an hour, not much progress had been made. Finally, the sales manager interrupted. Turning to the foundry executives, he suggested, "Look, why don't we simply mold the part in two pieces and send them to you. You can insert the core at the foundry and glue the two plastic halves together over it. That way we'll never have to see or handle the core."

Conversation froze in midair. "That's the answer," said a foundry engineer. He turned to the sales manager. "How the hell did you think of that? It's so simple, it's frightening."

"Easy," said the sales manager. "It seemed to me that, as you kept devising these clever ways to handle the core [problem], we were building in costs that eventually none of us could live with. I had visions of a canceled order [problem impact], so I figured it was time to take a good hard look at the source of these costs. So, while you were wondering what to do *with* the core [cause of the problem], I was thinking of what could be done *about* the core [cause of the problem impact]."

With his eye on the possible loss of business (the cost/profit-based problem impact), the sales manager was not limited by either constraint, enabling his range of thinking to expand beyond that of the engineers.

ANOTHER WHACK AT THE TWO CONSTRAINTS

This tendency to be hobbled by the two constraints diminishes further as we look at another super executive trait—the search for solution-totality. Chances are, if a problem has become repetitive in one form or another, then past attempts to solve it have been similarly repetitive in type and these efforts probably have been pretty well locked into a narrow, limited framework. If we ask the question "Are we simply nipping at the problem so we'll constantly have to react to it or are we trying to find a solution so we'll never have to see the damn thing again?" then it's pretty hard to be constrained by precedent or constants. Obviously, not every problem can be solved in one fell swoop so it never comes up again. Short of dynamiting the competitor's plant, the problem of suddenly finding a new competitor in a limited market can't always be whisked away in one step. A whole host of steps may be required to meet the threat. (If you do resort to dynamite, don't tell anyone you read about it here. I have enough problems.) For the record, I'd suggest cutting price, turning out a better product or marketing it better, or merging the two companies.

Most problems, however, do lend themselves to at least some prospect of solution-totality, *if* we're oriented toward thinking in these terms. For example, an indifferent labor force with product quality problems can be fussed at, punished, threatened, and reasoned with. This is the usual incremental-solution approach, and we usually accept the fact that the quality problem will come up again and again in one form or another and that the best we can hope for is that with luck we'll chip away at it. The precedent in this case is that this is the way we've always handled this problem, and the constant is an indifferent, perhaps intractable labor force, not subject to significant attitude change. If, on the other hand, we think in terms of solution-totality, we might try a completely new approach designed to wipe out the problem. One such approach might be a quality-circle program, involving both management and labor as partners rather than adversaries, and by so doing wiping out the precedent and the constant.

TIME

The economical use of time is another super executive trait that we can learn. Stalling is for most of us a kind of crutch. If we can't get a handle on a problem we say, "Let's talk about this later, O.K.?" Perhaps we hope the problem will magically disappear or correct itself or that somehow someone else will bang up against it and solve it. Or when we find it difficult to get galvanized into action, we talk about the complexity of today's organizations and simply rationalize, "Hell, these things take time." Or we suggest "Let's sleep on it awhile" when we can't make a decision. (The fact is the only decision most people make in their sleep is when to turn over.) Time crutches are insidious. The more we use them, the more we tend to rely on them. For many people, they often become a way of business life.

Forcing ourselves to compress time input has an additional advantage of limiting the amount of time we can spend on the tangential and peripheral, encouraging us to think in core terms. With most super executives, efficient use of time comes naturally. But once the principle is understood and appreciated, many non super executives, perhaps most, develop a pretty good work pattern of time compression. This happens through practice and even more so out of necessity, especially if the organizational environment is conducive to it. We'll go into this in detail in Part Two.

The president of a large distribution company asked me to review the work habits of his sales manager. A great salesman, sharply analytical, liked by his staff and salesmen, he could find 400 ways to put off making a decision, frustrating the hell out of his people as well as costing the company some good sales opportunities. As a result of confusing procrastination with prudence and giving the knee-jerk response "Later," he increasingly distrusted his first impulses. There seemed little question but that he knew what to do. He just had trouble telling others to do it. "Let me think about it" (he generally didn't), "I'll get back to you" (after a while, nobody hung by their thumbs waiting), "I can't decide until you get me such-and-such information" (a common delay mechanism), all substituted for decisions. If this continued, the president told me, it would probably cost the sales manager his job.

After I watched him in action as a silent observer for a couple of hours, the solution came to me. "Tell him," I suggested to the president, "that no one who comes into his office for an on-the-spot decision is to leave without it. Period." (I was, I must admit, highly embarrassed at the simplicity of the suggestion. It was my feeling that the problem wasn't incompetence. It was habit, and the best way to break a habit, according to my simple mind, is not to do it anymore. See how easy it is to be a consultant? Before I learned that super executives are simple and direct, I probably would have tried to be clever and to solve this problem by analyzing his motivations, setting up new reporting procedures, perhaps reorganizing the department, and maybe reorganizing the sales manager out of his job.)

The president so directed the sales manager. An on-the-spot decision was defined to him as one that could be made without further informational input. It was also suggested to him that anytime he was tempted to say "Later" he was to ask himself, "Why later? Why the hell not right now?" If there was any question, he was to err on the side of making a decision anyway. The jolt of suddenly finding himself under the gun in new, unfamiliar territory was wisely tempered by the president's assurance that the sales manager would not be faulted on the quality of his decisions, only for his failure to make them. "Somehow we'll keep score," the president told him. "If you don't make some mistakes, it'll be pretty clear to me that you're not making enough on-the-spot decisions."

It worked. Not only did the sales manager make faster, more incisive decisions, but he became more relaxed, no longer having the pressure of a pile of unmade decisions constantly in front of him and a lot of people on his back looking for them. As a corollary benefit, the decision-making pace of his people appeared to pick up also as the sales manager became less tolerant of any procrastination he noted on their part.

Although in this case the sales manager adapted to this super executive trait because it became a specific job requirement and he had the native ability to do it, the fact is many of us can infuse time-compression into our organizations to a greater degree than we think once we break the molds of inertia and old habits and red-flag the verbal time crutches that make putting things off until "later" so easy.

SUMMARY

What we can learn from the super executive rounds out like this:

We can learn to approach most problem and opportunity situations from the vantage point of their profit/cost-based problem impacts. This will be helped by relating more of our activities and decisions to our ultimate responsibility to make or save money rather than solely to our functional responsibilities.

We can shoot for more solution-totality in facing problems and opportunities. ("If we do what we propose doing, will we ever see this problem again in its present form?")

We can become more aware of how the two constraints of precedents and constants crimp our thinking and, once aware of this, work around them.

We can compress our time inputs from present levels to a point short of going off half-cocked, by recognizing the difference between rash impulsiveness and good sound use of time.

The more these qualities can be infused into the pattern of organizational thinking, the more an organization can respond to the total needs of problem and opportunity situations, and the more individual and organizational perspectives will be widened by the bigger picture built into the problem-impact approach.

And that's a whole lot better than a stick in the eye.

PART TWO

THE KEY TO MOVING FASTER

CHAPTER 3

What the Hell *Is* Tempo— And Why Is It So Important?

Several years ago, as the after-dinner speaker, I addressed a group of businessmen on the subject of organizational tempo. Afterward, the CEO of a machine tool company, who had perhaps wisely spent the evening at the bar, stopped me. With more curiosity than belligerence, he asked, "What the hell *is* tempo?"

Good question. But discerning a limited future in prolonging the conversation, I shrugged my shoulders. "Beats me," I told him. "Why the hell do you want to know?"

He paused, thought about it for a few moments, then shrugged his shoulders. "Beats me," he said, walking off.

But the question remains.

DEFINING TEMPO

Organizational tempo is the speed with which an organization moves, thinks, and gets things done; how fast it makes and implements decisions, reacts to new business climates, adapts to sudden shifts in the marketplace and competitive pressures, creates new products and services, solves problems, and seizes new opportunities. In short, it is the pulse of the organization!

Five quick facts about tempo:

Fact 1. Every organization has a tempo, and everything the organization does is done within the time frame established by that tempo. It is the pervasive climate in which the organization operates. An organization's tempo—good, bad, or indifferent—determines what that organization can accomplish in a given time period.

Fact 2. Next to making the right decisions, the speed with which those decisions are made has more to do with the success or failure of an organization than any other single factor!

Fact 3. Incredibly, despite the above, we generally do not think of an organization as having a tempo. In fact, we seldom think of tempo at all. Consequently, we seldom set out to do anything to improve it.

Fact 4. Slow tempo can occur at any and all levels. If it occurs significantly at top levels, the problem will tend to show up in bottom-line results and either the organization will go down the tube or top management will get axed.

At lower and middle levels of management, for reasons we'll go into later, slow tempo is usually just as damaging. Because we don't look for it, especially in these terms, it tends to be less obvious—and therefore more insidious. At these levels it can eat away, undetected, at the effectiveness of the whole organization.

Size is no protection against slow tempo. It can afflict any organization, from the one-man plumbing shop to the automotive giant. Obviously, when you're dealing with a very small organization, personal work habits and attitudes tend to be a dominant influence. As the organization gets larger, organizational structure becomes a progressively greater influence to be reckoned with.

Fact 5. Finally, *no* organization moves anywhere near its maximum potential tempo; therefore, every organization can improve its tempo. Bad can become good, and good can become better. The room for movement is as infinite as the *need* for improvement.

It's characteristic of our times that many old theories simply don't work anymore. New problems and new opportunities are surfacing in the 1980s that are of magnitudes unparalleled in the 1970s. The organization that isn't light on its feet, that can't respond quickly and decisively to the battering storms and transient new opportunities of the present and future, may not live too long or too successfully. The premium slow-tempoed organizations have to pay, regardless of their size, has simply gotten too high not to do something about it.

And that, dear reader, is essentially what the hell tempo is all about.

TEMPO IN ACTION

As managers, we're confronted daily with the need to make decisions and get things done. The following two situations are theoretical in name only. We wrestle with them or their hundreds of counterparts all the time. It's what most of us are paid to do.

One of your salesmen is hot on the trail of a large account. To get it, certain concessions—payment terms, perhaps—must be made. He asks your sales manager for permission to make them.

If the sales manager gets back to your salesman within a day or two, he'll probably have a pretty good shot at getting the account. Perhaps the cutting edge of his sales approach hasn't worn off the prospect, who would probably be impressed with your company's decisiveness and the fact that the man he'll be doing business with has enough clout to properly service the account.

But suppose the sales manager gets back to the salesman in two weeks with the same decision. There's a good chance the prospect might have lost interest or that the couple of weeks has given your competition time to react and put the skids

under your man. (Such are the unfortunate realities of corporate life that, after undermining the salesman's efforts by his
procrastination, the sales manager would plant the onus for
the loss smack on the shoulders of the salesman. The effect
would be, of course, that the issue would become the salesman's competence rather than the slow-tempoed response by
the sales manager.)

Let's take a longer term example: Your company decides to
expand its product line. The product has to be selected and
developed, the market researched, and marketing strategies
developed. Funds must be committed, and production facilities organized.

Throughout the whole process, a lot of people and many departments have to get involved. Meetings must be held, and
information gathered, analyzed, and coordinated. Many decisions, judgments, and actions are needed all along the path.
Each step has a time frame—the time it takes to perform that
step. There are time gaps in between in which nothing is being
done—dead time so far as the project is concerned. (We're
waiting for Harold to make a decision, and Harold is out of
town and won't be back until next Tuesday. Jasper has to come
up with some data, and he gets bogged down in an unfore-
seen crisis. Alfred has to make a decision and doesn't know
what to do, so he does nothing until someone twists his arm
or makes the decision for him. Bernard needs more and more
information, a seemingly endless supply of it, before he can
crank in his contribution.) The total of these time frames plus
the gaps in between is how long it takes to make the decision
and implement it.

Assuming you've made all the right moves and all the right
decisions, and your organization is geared to put all this together in, say, six months, you'll find one impact on your
company. Maybe you'll scoop your competition or hit the sea-
son just right.

But if the company's geared to take 18 months, you'll have

an entirely different impact. By that time, maybe your competition will have gone on the market first or perhaps whole generations of new products will have leapfrogged over yours, and all those right decisions and right moves will have *cost* your company money instead of making it money! Or perhaps neither of the above will occur, but if the product is successful, you still will have lost 12 months' profits on it. Further, if you're geared to 6 months, theoretically you could have gotten three new products on the market within the same 18-month period, not just one.

So, to restate the second fact about tempo: Assuming you make all the right decisions to solve a problem or take advantage of an opportunity, the effect of those decisions will depend primarily on the time frame in which they're made. And this is why an organization's success or failure hinges so critically on its tempo.

WHY HAVE WE IGNORED TEMPO?

If tempo is so bloody important, why have we pretended it doesn't exist? A fair question. Why can't we take a course, Tempo 1, in business schools? Why is the literature on the subject almost nonexistent? Why don't presidents of companies call meetings, pound their desks, get red in the face, and holler, "Our organization's tempo is terrible! Do something, dammit! Speed it up!"

All of us get frustrated from time to time when certain projects don't get off the ground, when particular decisions don't get made, when necessary feedback doesn't flow fast enough (or at all). Sometimes we feel like lighting a stick of dynamite under somebody. But we tend to show this frustration item by item, without recognizing that perhaps we're dealing with a systemic organizational defect.

And even in those rare cases where someone suggests,

"We're dead on our backsides. It takes us forever and two weeks to make a decision or to make a move. Something's wrong," the tendency is to blame individuals. Sometimes replacing those individuals reduces the problem. More often than not, however, the basic corporate environment remains the same (especially if top and top-middle management stays in place), and the new people, after perhaps making dynamic entrances, eventually melt into the existing tempo climate.

It is, when you think about it, incredible that tempo—such a vital part of the whole process of organizational effectiveness—is so little understood and so seldom addressed at the executive levels. (We know plenty about it at the lower plant levels. Ask any time-study man or manufacturing engineer who owns a clipboard and a stopwatch about pace and tempo, or any manufacturing executive with a production and cost readout, and you'll probably get a pretty detailed tour of the subject. But at the policy-making levels, where the character and personality of the organization is developed, the subject of organizational tempo usually draws blank stares and a "Huh?")

There are four reasons why tempo has been ignored at the executive levels, and understanding these reasons is important because, if we don't understand them, chances are we'll continue to ignore tempo.

Reason 1. This is the age of the computer. If we can't crank something into a computer, can't quantify it, can't build a model, all too often we assume that it doesn't exist—and we don't yet know how to crank tempo into a computer.

Organizationally, tempo is the product of cumulative work habits and patterns; to a large extent, it represents the philosophy and personality of the organization. As we've noted, it's a pervasive climate, and how do you measure a climate? Obviously, you can't in conventional terms. It's "faster" than what? Or "slower" than what?

And that's the problem. Where do you find the takeoff point, a standard against which to measure changes in tempo? Without one, we can't go any further. This failure to establish a starting point is what has kept business academics, management experts, and business managers from seriously addressing the subject. (Hang in there, because we've found that take-off point, and we'll discuss it in a later chapter.)

Reason 2. Most top managers think they're fast paced and action oriented and assume that, if they are, then the organization, reflecting its leadership, will be also.

The first premise has a kernel or two of truth. Not many people get to be top managers by wasting time and letting events control *them*.

The second premise? Not so true. What goes in at the top doesn't always come out the same way at the bottom. As policy and project decisions drift down the organizational pyramid, the friction inherent in any movement tends to inhibit them. For example, a lack of full understanding of the policy or project and its nuances, or a diminishing intensity of interest and enthusiasm (a phenomenon that occurs in direct proportion to the distance from where the project was decided on), or a simple inability to translate the intent into the full scope of action are all likely to be inhibitory. Pockets of slow decision making relating to implementation create further impediments. (We'll discuss these in more detail in the next chapter.)

The fact is top managers don't usually consider tempo as an important *organizational* problem because their perspective is different from that of people at levels where slow tempo exists in its most insidious form. Top managers are generally insulated from lower levels by their different functions and responsibilities, by intervening layers of management, and often by muddied decision-making responsibilities along the line.

This insulation tends to breed ignorance, which in turn breeds indifference. The result: Top management generally has a blind spot when it comes to the orientations of the rest of the organization, and tempo is one of these orientations, perhaps the most important.

Reason 3. We are victims as well as beneficiaries of the Protestant Ethic. At the executive level, we equate hard work with long hours of effort, not with *rate of accomplishment*—and there's a big difference!

In an attempt to accomplish more, we tend to increase working hours rather than speed up our pace, and this reliance on long hours to make up the gap often covers up a slow tempo—indeed, it often *contributes* to it.

For example, Paul Poof, a department head, has a slow productive pace. Perhaps he diddles and fusses (looking real busy while he does it) when he should be making decisions or spends an inordinate amount of time putting together an overkill of data, checking and rechecking it, in a vain attempt to take all the risk out of the decisions he does make. To try to accomplish what he's paid to accomplish, he works 10–11 hours a day, takes a full briefcase home every night, and is often found at his desk on Saturday morning, tie askew, poring over papers, a cup of stale coffee by his side. We consider Paul a hero, giving his all in an inspirational effort for dear old Doofuncky Corp.

Paul is no hero. By extending his working day, chances are he, like many of us, is successfully masking a tempo problem. His rate of accomplishment has stretched (slowed) so that what he should do in 8 hours he is doing in say 10 hours. But his department is geared for an 8-hour day, and it tends to adapt to the slower rate. Result: His department can run at four-fifths or less of the speed it should. (In practice, Paul will probably inveigle or cajole some of his executive troops to put in long hours, too. Now you've got a whole department feeling sorry for itself or feeling frustrated while at the same time spinning a lot of unproductive wheels in the process.)

In any event, the ready availability of more hours for "hard work" has helped us ignore the subject of tempo (read: "rate of accomplishment").

Reason 4. Finally, we assume that our collective and individual paces, if we even think about them, which is doubtful, are "normal." After all, we are what we are; our organization is what it is. This is how we function. Our work pattern has always been this way. Everyone seems to be working diligently. We have nothing to measure it against, so we don't think about our tempo being right or wrong, slow or fast.

If we wake up in the morning with no headache, we don't think about *not* taking an aspirin. Similarly, if we consider something normal, we tend not to do anything about it and not to recognize that perhaps something has gone awry.

Ergo, we tend to ignore this whole critical problem of organizational tempo.

THE KEY TO MEASURING TEMPO

O.K., so now we've defined tempo, made some judgments about it and its critical influence on every organization, and figured out why we've ignored it up till now. But the problem still remains. How do we measure it or somehow get a handle on it so we can have something tangible to remold?

The primary function of every organization is to make decisions and then implement them. Nothing happens in any organization (unless you consider vegetation as a happening) until someone makes a decision to do something. (Yes, dear reader, we could say that making no decision is a decision not to do anything, but let's think positively.) The key to understanding and measuring tempo lies, therefore, in the speed with which our decision-making processes work. Measure that, and chances are we'll get a pretty good handle on our tempo. (Naturally, the speed of implementation is also a factor. But for now, consider implementation as nothing more than the product of a series of decisions, and while an organization can stumble and bumble along in the implementation phase, chances are that, if it is fast paced in its decision making, implementation will follow at the same pace.)

In any event, once we identify what elements slow the decision-making process (which we'll talk about in the next chapter), we can then measure our organization's tempo against what it can or should be (see the chapter after that), and finally, armed with that knowledge, we can do something about it (see the chapter after that). All of this leads to the final desired result: a stepped-up tempo, with more organizational accomplishment in less time.

OOPS, ANOTHER PROBLEM

But first, we've got to overcome another barrier—complacency. We've been lulled into this state of complacency, not only by the four reasons we've already noted, but also by the fact that the present system for making decisions *should* work. Theoretically, our formally structured organization tables, with their neat squares and straight lines, with staff and line responsibilities and profit centers spelled out, create the power points, networks, and lines of communication for good timely decision making.

But something happens between theory and practice. And what happens is *people*. We assume that the people in our organization have certain strengths, and our decision-making processes are built around these strengths—ambitiousness, competence, action orientation, and the like. But people also have certain weaknesses. And these weaknesses, unless something is done about them, tend to reinforce themselves, often reducing the decision-making process, or segments of it, to a shambles.

Unfortunately, we seldom take these weaknesses into account in designing our decision-making processes. Yet to maximize the effectiveness of these processes, to get them into high gear tempo-wise, we must somehow compensate for them and, where possible, change organizational structure to eliminate their effects.

Before we get into this restructuring, let's take a look at these weaknesses—what they are, how they enter the process, and how they negatively impact on our organizational tempo.

CHAPTER 4

Decision Making and People Weaknesses

A fable to illustrate a point:

The VP of Whatever walked into his president's office. "President," he said, "I have a great idea. Our business is selling food to pet alligators—namely, horsemeat, which is getting in short supply. Why don't we sell ground-up dog meat, which alligators like very much, since there seems to be an abundance of dogs, judging by the mess on my front lawn."

"Great idea!" said the president, patting the VP on the head. "Let's proceed at once! Round up the dogs!"

At the same time, a thousand miles away on the edge of the Florida Everglades, another VP strode into his boss's office. "Boss," he said, "I have a great idea. We sell dog food—namely, horsemeat, which is getting in short supply. Why don't we grind up alligators, which dogs would like very much, since there seems to be an abundance of alligators, judging by the number on my front lawn."

"Maybe," said the boss. "Let's call a meeting of department heads for next Tuesday." But on Monday, the head of marketing found that he had to address a convention of the American Association of English Bulldog Owners and Lovers Thereof (or "AAOEBOALT" as it is called), so the meeting was postponed until a week from Thursday.

At the meeting, there was a lot of hesitation over whether

alligator was really the way to go. "After all," said the head of R&D, "It's never been done before."

"Very well," said the boss, "let's research the market." So two weeks later, they ground up a somewhat reluctant alligator and polled some dogs, who, judging from the way they wolfed it down, loved it. They called another meeting for the next Wednesday to discuss the results, but the meeting had to be postponed until a week from Friday because the head of marketing got bitten on the butt by a hungry Great Dane while doing his market research and couldn't sit down for a while.

"Can our production facilities handle alligator meat?" asked the boss of his production manager at the meeting. "Don't know," said the latter. "I'll start thinking about it." "How about an advertising campaign?" the boss asked his advertising manager. "We'll discuss it with our agency, which unfortunately is going to be tied up for two weeks," replied the latter. "But don't worry, we'll put together a boffo campaign that will have every dog in America champing to chomp alligator."

"Great!" said the boss. "We're really moving right along."

Alas, shortly thereafter, while the head of production was still thinking about it and the advertising manager was waiting for the agency and various other executives were doing their things, the VP again walked into his boss's office. "Boss," he said, "we're in big trouble. While we have been considering grinding up alligators for the dog food market, the alligator food people have been grinding up our market—namely dogs. We are out of business."

Moral: Slow decision making is the best way for a company to go to the dogs.

Having established the importance of tempo (in Chapter 3), let's now take a look at how some of the people weaknesses we referred to contribute to a slow decision-making process—

a condition that is both a manifestation and the primary source of slow organizational tempo. And, pursuing that finely honed logic, if we can lick some of the problems of slow decision making, we will essentially have licked a good part of the problem of slow organizational tempo and vice versa. We will, of course, first have to bring into focus what it is that impacts negatively on the process.

THE EFFECT OF PEOPLE WEAKNESSES—AN OVERVIEW

So what follows is what happens when we crank people, with all their strengths and foibles, into the decision-making process. As we tick off the effects, you may shrug your shoulders, scratch your head, and grumble cynically, "Come on now. This simply wouldn't happen in any kind of sophisticated organization. If it does, somebody isn't paying attention." Or you might take the opposite and more common tack and say, "Well, yes . . . but this happens to some extent in *every* organization. After all, people are people [now there's a profound observation], and you have to expect some of this."

Agreed. Some or all of what follows does occur in every organization, either in pockets or systemically. That's a given. In fact, if you make the effort, you'll probably have little trouble identifying each item we tick off with some segment of your own organization. But the other viewpoint is also correct. Somebody isn't paying attention, which is precisely our point. No one pays attention to a problem until that problem is recognized as a problem, and slow tempo, which can't be quantified in absolute terms, does a great job of blending in with the wallpaper. Ask any manager what his problems are and he'll tell you about shortages, the high cost of money, intransigent labor, competitive price cutting, and production breakdowns, but seldom, if ever, will he identify his organization's tempo as one of those problems—even though tempo is what determines how fast his organization will handle these other problems. Another thing that makes slow tempo less visible as a problem is the fact that the very hustle and bustle of any organization that devotes most of its efforts to running its daily operations, putting out obvious or immediate fires, and trying to latch onto fleeting opportunities tends to mask many organizational defects, especially if these defects are organizational climates, such as slow tempo.

Second, yes, "you have to expect some of this." O.K., but how much? I don't want to overstate the case. If *every* facet of *every* organization operated totally in the manner I'll be outlining, we'd all be back to pounding wheels out of stone. But bear in mind that this chapter is devoted to what can and does go wrong with our decision-making processes, not what's right with them. Obviously, there's plenty right. Our goal is simply to unmask the wrong, to put it in a perspective where it can be identified and then dealt with.

The point is that all organizations, the effective ones and the ones not so effective, develop patterns of behavior that tend to become accepted as normal for those organizations. Occasionally, some aspect of them irritates and frustrates us, and we resolve to correct it. But we often do this without realizing that, in the case of slow tempo, we're dealing with *basic* attitudes and undercurrents that flow through the organization that go well beyond the one or two manifestations we may sporadically address. These undercurrents and attitudes form an operating environment, and even an organization with a good growth rate and heady profits inherently operates in an environment that puts some checks on its achieving even more growth and more profitability. In other organizations (to go to the other end of the spectrum), this environment can flat-out cripple the organization without anyone fully realizing what it is that did the crippling. As I was told by the president of one defunct company that had a severe slow decision-making problem that wasn't recognized until too late, "We knew what to do. That wasn't our problem. Somehow, we just couldn't seem to pull it all together and decide to get it done.''

So again, how much should we expect? The answer depends on how much we do to control the problem. The more effective action we take, the less we should expect and the more our operating environment will tend to tilt toward the success end of the scale. The more complacently we accept the problem as ''one of those things every company has to live with'' and the less effort we apply as a result, the more the scale will tip the other way.

Another point. Slow decision making obviously can (and does) occur at every level of management. However, we'll be concentrating more on the middle and lower levels, because this is where, as noted before, the problem is less obvious and thus more insidious. Lower levels are, in a sense, the operating levels, the levels at which policy is translated into action. A cumbersome, ponderous decision-making process at these levels cannot help but impact on the organization's vitality and its overall achievement.

THE ELEVEN ELEMENTS OF SLOW DECISION MAKING

Timidity

You're managing a team locked in a pennant race. Crucial game. Two out. Ninth inning. Three men on. Three and two count on your batter. You're losing 1 to 0. The tension mounts. A hush falls over the crowd. The pitcher winds up and grooves a home-run ball right down the middle. Your batter simply watches it go by. The crowd groans. Game's over.

Head down, dejected, the batter shuffles back to the dugout. While two coaches and a batboy restrain you, you scream, ''Why didn't you at least swing at it?'' Digging his toe into the ground, he mutters, ''I was afraid I'd miss.''

That's timidity, perhaps the greatest deterrent to fast, incisive decision making. In business it translates into the concept that *no* decision is better and safer than any decision. And more and more executives are operating under the theory that, the fewer controversial decisions they make, the less chance they will have to accept responsibility for a wrong one.

Timidity can stem from many diverse sources. The most common is the fear of making a mistake and having to face its possible consequences or the fear of doing something that might change an otherwise comfortable or acceptable status quo. For example, getting bounced out for coming up with a big blooper can pretty much change the status quo for the worse. So does getting a demotion or losing prestige or being consulted less.

Timid executives are generally defensive ones. You tell one that someone goofed in the Oshgosh plant a thousand miles away and his first reaction is "Don't blame me! I didn't do it!" These are the people who when presented with a problem devote more energy and cleverness to proving they didn't cause it than to trying to solve it. They simply don't want to be associated with failure, or possible failure, and making decisions, of course, always runs some risk of failure. So not only do they themselves shy away from making decisions but, if they have managerial control over others, their attitude tends to make those others timid also.

Timid executives generally lean toward making highly defensible decisions, often slowing the process to a snail's pace while they try to amass all kinds of supportive data and to get as many people as possible to back their conclusions. Then if something doesn't work out right, they're ready with a "See, it wasn't my fault" defense.

As some executives approach retirement, especially those in key middle-management positions, they may walk on eggs to avoid jeopardizing that future good life of rocking on the porch, sipping martinis, waiting for the mailman to round the corner with their pension checks. When one or two of these people, having gone as far in the organization as they can reasonably expect, are strategically placed, this cautious attitude often bottlenecks the decision-making process.

Where real hardball executive competition exists or departmental prerogatives are overzealously guarded or the organization is splintered with competing factions, all this can manifest itself by people trying to avoid making mistakes (avoiding decisions) rather than by scoring points by positive accomplishment (making decisions). Most executives operate most comfortably in an atmosphere of unanimity. They delay making a decision in the face of conflict or critical opposition simply because it is disquieting or unpleasant. Often where there is conflict, they may drag their heels hoping that somehow as time passes unanimity will be achieved either by persuasion or by a change in the circumstances on which this contentious decision was to have been based.

Some top managements, out of either impatience or arrogance, create an environment in which mistakes by others (never themselves) are viewed solely as criteria for performance rather than as a basis for learning. This is sure to breed timidity into the organization. It's pretty hard for an executive to concentrate on making good, creative, innovative decisions—ones that perhaps call for some bridge burning or for committing large chunks of money—when he knows that his job or career is on the line with each decision. Timidity *has* to be infused into an organization's personality by an environment that says, "O.K., fella, one strike and sayonara." A supportive organization says, "Look, your reasoning made sense. You faced up to the problem and that's good. Unfortunately, it just didn't work out. Nice try. Let's learn from it. Undo it as best you can, and better luck next time." An organization that goes about on tiptoes or is constantly looking over its shoulder tends to move slowly, if at all.

Often an executive fears that a subordinate's mistake might

reflect adversely on him and doesn't consider that having a subordinate willing to attack a problem may be a credit to him. Such an executive may build timidity into his staff by constantly operating in a panic and by his unreasonable harshness with anyone making a mistake or a wrong decision, no matter how well intentioned. Others might want to make all the decisions themselves yet retain the facade of delegation so if one turns out wrong they can shift the blame. This "heads I win, tails you lose" business causes many subordinate executives to tread warily.

The list of timidity sources is endless, but the results are pretty much the same. Decisions drift while the decision maker tries to dodge the decision or to get someone else to share responsibility in case it turns out wrong. Or he may try to shift the blame for delay elsewhere. Meanwhile, the decision isn't made. And even when it is, timidity can leave its stamp on the nature of the decision itself—safe and conservative and perhaps not fully responsive to the problem or opportunity— all of which means that very likely even more time and energy will have to be redevoted to it later.

We've mentioned skirting and evading decisions several times, so let's digress for a few moments to talk about this business of ducking decisions. In many organizations, as many decisions are ducked as are made. Some people can thread their way around a decision-making responsibility like an all-pro running back picking his way downfield.

Evasion can be simple and subtle. For example, before a meeting breaks, someone brings up a new subject. It's discussed for a few minutes, then the meeting ends with the statement, "All right, John, think about it and then let's do something." John, who is charged with thinking about it and then doing something, does neither, gambling that there's a very good chance it will never be brought up again, especially if it seems like just an afterthought in a meeting that involved many other things. That's one form of evasion.

Another very common technique is based on a fact of organizational life, that a decision will tend to gravitate to the highest level that gets involved. Let's say an industrial engineer brings a problem to the head of industrial engineering for a decision. The latter, who is responsible for making the decision, decides, for whatever reason, he doesn't want to touch it. So he finds the opportunity to casually bring it up with the plant manager: "Say, what do you think?" Invariably, the plant manager will either make the decision or take it a step further. The plant manager that same day has a meeting with the VP of manufacturing to discuss next year's budget. In the course of conversation, he casually mentions the problem: "I've got this little problem. . . ." You can bet that the decision will be made right there by the VP. He makes a "suggestion" ("If it were me, I think I'd. . . .") Everyone is now happy, especially the head of engineering, who very neatly evaded making the decision. The sad part is neither the VP nor the plant manager ever realized that they were trapped into making a decision one or two levels above where it should have been made by the guy getting paid to make it. What suffered? Time (that is, tempo), perhaps the quality of the decision, and certainly the ability of the organization to act effectively and decisively.

Here's another technique: The decision maker asks a whole slew of people for data and recommendations that he supposedly needs to make his decision. Out of the crowd, one or two are bound not to respond, people who are perhaps busy with their own problems and who won't move until pushed. So the decision maker simply doesn't push. Result: The decision drags, and if the decision maker is suddenly confronted with the fact that he hasn't attacked the problem, he simply says, "I'm still waiting for so-and-so to get back to me with some information I need. I don't know why the hell it should take him so long." Or he might on a few occasions say to the tardy colleague, "When you get a chance, let me have your thoughts on such-and-such." Since there's no urgency in his voice, the colleague promptly dismisses the request as not too important. Now the decision maker can say, "I've asked him repeatedly for his recommendation." In any event, he'll try to buy more time and then lay the responsibility for delay on the other guy.

Here's an example of decision evasion in action:

A division of a multibillion-dollar electronics conglomerate, a company that prides itself, with justification, on its organizational and management excellence, developed a specialized computer. To ship the computer, it needed a shipping package. The alternatives came down to two: an inexpensive molded plastic package requiring a $5,900 mold, and an expensive fabricated package requiring no mold. The first year's production estimate indicated that the difference in part price would mean a saving of $18,000 going the molded route. If production increased as expected, so would the savings.

A simple decision? Seemingly. Everyone involved—the packaging engineer, his boss, the head of traffic, and the production manager—agreed that the molded pack was the way to go, but it also meant someone had to O.K. a purchase order for the mold. When it came time to put signature to paper, suddenly everybody was out to lunch. Signatures after all mean commitments, and commitments could spell trouble if something goes wrong—especially if it involves a $5,900 lump-sum investment.

What to do? First step: Send the purchase order to the plant manager for his signature, and hope he'll relieve the pressure. Nice try, but no dice. He bounces it back: "You guys decide." Second step: By tacit agreement, delay the decision until it becomes too late to order a mold (10 weeks delivery). They would then be forced to go to the more quickly available fabricated pack, which, although more expensive, required no initial large investment for a mold.

This is a classic case of "It shouldn't have happened," especially in such a well-run, sophisticated, and successful company. But it did, and no red flags were ever raised. (Six years and about $410,000 later, a new packaging engineer finally rammed through a switch to a molded pack.) Bear in mind that this was not an earth-shaking decision. In fact, in a company this size, it could be scored as a minor one to be made at relatively low levels. It never did reach higher echelons, where the ploy might have been detected—although even that is unlikely.

Consider now the vast number of other "minor" decisions that are either evaded or delayed in the course of everyday operations in virtually every business organization; the cost, if it could be measured in dollars, could be staggering. This points up the insidiousness of deferred and evaded decision making and the influence of slow tempo on the bottom line. Evasion techniques are varied and countless. They're sometimes subtle, often blatant, but on the whole they tend to work because we aren't normally sensitive to the undercurrents of timidity and inaction ebbing and flowing through our organizations.

With that happy thought in mind, let's return to those elements that create havoc on the decision-making process.

Incompetence

Incompetence, which in a sense is related to timidity, is another major cause of slow decision making. If an executive is faced with a problem and simply doesn't know what to do about it (or lacks the confidence that he knows what to do about it), chances are he'll try everything not to expose this. He might ignore the problem, try to minimize its seriousness, or find all kinds of excuses to delay dealing with it. Meanwhile the problem lives on, often getting worse, until perhaps a crisis forces someone to do something.

When they can't find anyone else to make the decision, and

they get backed into a decision-making corner, incompetent people (and we're not talking about those who get jammed up from time to time on a problem, as we all do, but those who are flat-out incapable of handling their jobs) almost by definition make incompetent decisions. These often have to be reversed, corrected, or halted in midstream. This eats up time and overburdens the decision-making process, since additional decisions are then needed to deal with the foul-ups caused by the original decision.

Vague Decision-Making Responsibility

Even in companies with very sophisticated tables of organization, it's not always clear which person is supposed to make the decision. Often a lot of time is lost while the decision goes looking for someone to make it.

Decisions that cut across departmental lines often cause a lot of confusion. For instance, take the simple selection of a new product package. Who will make the final decision—the marketing manager, who must sell the product and may want to use the package as a selling device, or the production manager, whose sole interest is to complete the product for shipping with the least cost and effort? These two people will have entirely different criteria as to what makes a good package. Confusion can reign while their different viewpoints are sorted out and composed and while both jockey to protect their departments' interests and to become the dominant influence over the final decision.

A company can experience shifting tides of corporate decision-making authority. For example, a new president with a marketing background can give, informally perhaps, more authority, credence, and clout to his marketing-oriented people, who talk his language. He might establish pipelines to top management for them outside the regular channels that were the prerogatives of, say, the manufacturing people under the old president. In the confusion (and confusion inevitably means time delay), subordinate executives are left to sort out the real power centers and to find which button to push to generate some movement.

In some fast-growing companies, responsibility vacuums develop and gaps appear in the decision-making process, making it unclear who is to make certain decisions. Or a man gets transferred or fired and, before his replacement is named, more gaps are created and decision-making responsibilities are shuffled around. These tend to take a set, so that when the new man comes aboard he's not too sure what he's responsible for.

Or the president casually sits in on a marketing meeting called to discuss a decision in the process of being made, one that's usually made by the marketing manager. The president, in offering "advice and suggestion," actually makes the decision. What happens the next time a similar problem comes up? This can be tricky if the marketing manager, who's perhaps closer to the problem, knows that his decision might run counter to the intent of the president's original decision.

Or an executive who has no trouble making decisions is consulted on a problem that is actually someone else's responsibility. He makes the decision this one time—and the next, and then the next. Pretty soon it's just assumed the decision-making responsibility is his. Or is it? Perhaps at one point he makes a decision that offends the person whose original responsibility it was and the latter attempts to reassert his "right" to make it. Confusion.

Or a "weak" executive, who over a period of time has either abdicated some of his decision-making authority or seen it eroded by "stronger," more forceful executives, is replaced by someone who tries to reassert that authority as part of his job. Battle lines are drawn and noses bent out of shape. Who will make the decision and, just as important, make it stick becomes cloudy.

Final decisions are often made by assent. Sales wants to change a component in a current product to increase its salability. It makes the decision to do so. Production must assent (when it gets around to it) to produce the component, which means that production actually makes the final decision, even though it is not subject to the same time pressure as sales.

The possibilities for confused lines of responsibility are endless, even with tightly drawn tables or organization. The net effect is that often decisions hang in limbo waiting for someone to make them and, worse yet, the door is open to anyone looking for a way to avoid making a decision.

Decision Drift

Here we come to one of the biggies in the list of causes of slow tempo. When the time frame for making a decision is *not* unequivocally spelled out, the result can be a problem that lives too long or an opportunity that comes and goes—that is, a dragged out decision. In a variation of Parkinson's Law, the time needed to make a decision expands so as to fill the time available for making the decision. This gives rise to an organizational phenomenon, "decision drift." This condition is as common as it is insidious; it's rooted in the fact that the time spent making a decision often bears little relationship to the time needed for the decision to be made. For example, a decision requiring an input of perhaps five or ten serious hours can take three or four months, and in retrospect, nobody knows why or just what the hell happened. The difference between the five or ten hours and the three or four months is *decision drift!*

But in our organizational wisdom, we explain this away in a phrase that is the most often used, all-inclusive, least questioned rationale for slow decision making: "These things take time." When this phrase becomes commonly accepted (as it generally is), the result is that nobody seriously pushes anyone else, and as time drags, initial feelings of urgency and enthusiasm are lost. In putting the decision together, somehow *tomorrow*, not today, becomes the target date for the next step. Minor stumbling blocks seem to grow into major crises as time passes, pushing the decision even further away. Storm into someone's office and ask, "Where the the hell is that information I asked for six weeks ago?" and he looks up with a pained smile and replies softly, "Hey, these things take time." When he shakes his head at the same time, indicating he doesn't understand why you don't understand that very basic principle of organizational life, your complaint is apt to hang in midair.

In larger companies, we accept the phrase because of the complexity of the organization, the many people that must get involved, the complexity and often magnitude of the decision itself, and its impact on various components of the organization. In smaller companies, we accept it because there are so few executives and they wear so many hats and are seemingly inundated by an accumulation of decision-making responsibilities. The process feeds on itself. The more unmade decisions there are floating around, without firm unequivocal time frames, the more difficult it becomes to make any decisions, as the whole process gets clogged up.

The amount of decision drift in any organization at any one time would probably stagger its management team if it could be accurately measured. The number of those decisions that could be finalized within 24 hours if someone seriously wanted or *had* to finalize them might also be a shocker.

Remote Decision Maker

Often the managers charged with making a decision can be a considerable distance from the heart of the problem or opportunity. They frequently lack the sense of urgency that someone

closer to it would have, underestimate the decision's importance, and lose sight of its nuances.

For example, the interest of a marketing manager whose
background is in advertising may lean toward selecting advertising media. He's less apt to be interested in solving a problem involving salesmen's morale, since, unlike the sales manager, he is one step removed from this. The result is that often
a decision regarding a more urgent and perhaps more immediate problem is allowed to drift, and this creates pockets of
slow decision making.

Loss of Decision-Making Momentum

Often a decision starts out like a ball of fire, then suddenly
loses its momentum, slows to a crawl, and sometimes stops
entirely. In most organizations, certain decisions must be
passed up the chain of command for approval or contributions
along the way. Sometimes so many people get involved that it
can take two computers and a mule named Benny to find who
is waiting for whom to take the next step. A decision can drift,
even get lost, simply because it's not equally important to
everyone along the chain. When it hits a pocket of comparative indifference, zonko, it can rattle around there, maybe never
again to see the light of day, unless perhaps a crisis impels
someone to try to rescue it.

When the chemistry is right, consensus is unquestionably
the best way to make decisions. Unfortunately, the chemistry
isn't always right, and when it isn't or when the attempt at
consensus involves too many people, then committee decisions can put the brakes on fast decision making. For example,
the often numerous meetings designed to reach consensus may
stretch out over a long period of time simply because it's hard
to get a whole bunch of people together at the same time and
then frequently it's necessary to reassemble later for more data

input and discussion. Then all too often a meeting is called and opinions are sought and some of those attending hide behind silence or vagueness, or offer a whole host of alternatives in the hope that maybe one will be right. Or they wait to see which way the boss leans so they can lean with him or which way the consensus is developing so they can climb aboard at the right time. Others may try to throw up some roadblocks, far-out irrelevant negatives that no one else thought of, in an effort to assert their independence or to show how perceptive they are. As a result, meetings can become inconclusive and repetitive with the obvious impact on the organization's tempo.

(In any event, committees have developed one fascinating type of person, the guy who has developed an extraordinary ability to associate himself with decisions that turn out right and disassociate himself from those that don't—all without ever firmly committing himself. Keep your eye on this fellow. He's destined for big things!)

Improper Delegation

Improper delegation breaks down into three basic categories. The first, and most obvious, is when the nominal delegator simply doesn't delegate. His subordinates are relegated to performing routine tasks, getting data for the delegator's decisions, and going for coffee. This fellow has a thing about accumulating responsibilities. He often goes about with furrowed brow, huffing and puffing about how busy he is, and putting in a whole lot of overtime hours, complaining bitterly, yet loving every minute of it. Because the number of decisions to be made piles up, he finds he can devote little time to any one decision. He often ends up making only those with which he is most comfortable, sloughing off others and making still others only when forced to by a crisis. I won't belabor this fellow's contribution to the erosion of an effective organization.

The second type of improper delegation occurs when a person delegates responsibility but holds tight to the reins while the subordinate struggles to hold up his end of the responsibility. The delegator is constantly evaluating procedures, approaches, and methods instead of results. This can be subtle: "Edgar, what are you doing about getting the loading dock doors replaced? I see. Why don't you call in so-and-so and see what he thinks [up to this point this is guidance], and—er— let me know what he says." This last is the kicker, the continued involvement in how Edgar manages to get the doors replaced. Edgar, who may feel he has the situation under pretty tight control, now has to stop, maybe reverse his field, and run the course outlined by the delegator, who in his own way simply doesn't want to let go.

Or it can be blatant: "Edgar, I want you to get the loading doors replaced. Now first, call in so-and-so. Then check to see what it would cost if our own people did it. Then. . . . Then. . . ." Edgar has not really been delegated a responsibility, just a series of tasks. While to the world Edgar is in charge of getting the damn doors replaced, in truth the delegator has never really let go.

The third category is when the person delegates but to the wrong people, to people who simply do not have the experience or the smarts to carry out the responsibility. Or the delegator might just lack the patience or know-how to guide his subordinates or to follow up properly. Whatever, he usually ends up doing the job himself or standing by while it doesn't get done or gets done wrong. Sometimes, perhaps totally subconsciously, a person delegates to the wrong people so that he can prove how essential he is when he has to rush to the rescue. Or perhaps he hasn't put together a competent staff or trained them properly or defined the job to be done with much clarity. In any event, he is a terrible manager of other people, and the tempo of the organization suffers.

Lack of Authority to Fully Control the Decision

Virtually every business manager pays homage to the principle of "authority commensurate with responsibility." Stack that up against motherhood, apple pie, and baseball, and it will win every time. But unfortunately, in practice it can quickly dissolve into myth.

Making a decision involves many steps: identifying and analyzing the problem or opportunity; garnering information (ranging from background to projections), opinions, and recommendations from others; compiling and sorting out alternative courses of action; engaging in creative thought; sometimes obtaining approval; and so on.

Most executives at subordinate levels simply lack the clout to get whatever inputs they need from others *when* they need them, especially if these people are in other departments or are superiors. It's pretty hard, for example, to storm into a superior's office, sweep his feet off his desk, and say, "Look, I asked you for your recommendations on this matter two weeks ago. A very simple request. But somehow you couldn't find the time? That's it, I need your answer in 15 minutes."

People have differet priorities, and this can get in the way when others are needed to supply data. What may be urgent to the decision maker isn't necessarily so to everyone else. They've got their own problems. Or if they're called on to help with a decision by making a firm recommendation, they often take the unspoken, if not subconscious, attitude of "Hell, that's his decision, not mine. If I go out on a limb and it works, most likely I'll get stiffed when the credit is handed out. But if I'm wrong, you can bet I'll get tagged as the scapegoat. No thanks!" Or if the decision will eventually affect them, their recommendations may be safe ones, lessening their subsequent risk and effort. Result: The people asked to contribute to the decision often drag their feet.

In short, good data and firm recommendations are often necessary ingredients of many decisions, and the inability of some decision makers to control the time gaps, let alone the content, takes a toll on the decision-making process.

Corporate Politics and Factionalism

We've already touched on corporate politics and factionalism in our discussion of timidity, but it merits a few paragraphs of its own. "Corporate politics and factionalism" has an ominous ring. We conjure up all kinds of mental pictures—of executives skulking in dark corners ready to gun down a rival for the next promotion opening, or of two executives jostling each other to grab the chair next to the VP of Whatever at lunch, or of one executive subtly sabotaging another's pet project, or, more realistically, of factions fighting to protect their points of view or for control over certain projects and decision areas and in the process putting the brakes on a lot of forward progress.

Admittedly, sometimes playing corporate politics is the only recourse open to a smart executive to make an end run around a boss who, for whatever reason, is purposely holding him and his ideas back. Sometimes it's the only way to move a project off dead center or to force a good idea into being seriously considered. Often it's the only way for a person with ambition to make his presence known. And often the procedures to resolve honest differences of opinion are so wishy-washy—or, more likely, the guy supposed to settle these differences is so wishy-washy—that both sides are forced to play politics.

But obviously, politics can also retard the decision-making process. Often the intensity of political infighting results in the political process becoming an end, not the means, and the infighting becomes more a device to simply establish a power position than to get things done.

For many executives, especially at lower levels, the atmosphere of political opposition negates an environment conducive to a free and easy flow of decision making. These people hold back either because of the unpleasantness they know will follow or because of conflicting instructions, or they try to wait to see which side is going to end up the most influential, or they take an inordinate amount of time to make highly defensible just-in-case decisions. The ramifications of organizational politics and factionalism are tricky, and in most cases, they work against the cause of good tempo.

Long Lead Times between Decisions and Implementation

Implementation of a decision is essentially the last part of the decision-making process, and it too has an obvious impact on organizational tempo. An organization can zip through a decision like a hot knife through butter, but if someone doesn't act on it, how fast the decision was made doesn't mean a thing.

Every organization develops patterns of time gaps between decisions and implementation, and these vary widely from company to company, department to department, and individual to individual. In some organizations, once a decision is reached, if a date (usually a tight date) is not set for implementation, it is understood that it begins immediately. In others, the attitude is "O.K., we made the decision, now let's implement it—when we get the chance." (The old standby "These things take time" applies to implementation with as much force, if not more, as it does to getting the basic decision made.) And even if a date is set for implementation in this type of company, excuses for missing the target date, usually some comfortable time in the future, are often accepted at the drop of a hat.

However, when we encourage or tolerate long lead times, a lot of other things happen—all geared to further slow tempo.

For one thing, people who start out all excited by the decision quickly lose this initial enthusiasm in geometric proportion to the time gap between decision and start of implementation. And unexcited people are seldom in a hurry. Further, in the absence of a tight time limit, expressed or implied, there is less need for innovation and creativity in taking the simplest, fastest, most direct route to implementation. The resultant slower routes further impinge on the organization's tempo in addition to dulling, through disuse, innovative and creative skills, which are the hallmarks of a fast-paced organization.

Another result: The longer the lead times, the more prone the implementers are to "work" the implementation into their daily routines. Say Herman, a marketing manager, works 50 hours a week supervising existing programs. Give him more or less work, he'll still fill his 50 hours. Now suddenly give him a month to find a new advertising agency, and he'll compress his work load or reprioritize it to make time for this new project. But give him six months to complete the same project, and his tendency is to "work" it into his daily routine. But he's already filling his 50 hours and somehow he can't really find the time, so this added project gets put off and delayed and doesn't seem to get into high gear. Tempo gets clobbered.

Organizational Personality

Every organization has its own unique personality and character. This is made up of many components, such as its traditions and philosophies; the attitudes, orientations, and work habits of its executive team; the energy levels and forcefulness or its top management; its general level of competence and aggressiveness; the attitude of its work force toward its jobs and its loyalty to the organization. Even its industry contributes to the organization's personality. A garment manufacturer, for example, because of the rough competitive nature of its industry and its need to respond to sudden market shifts, is apt to be more direct, lighter on its feet, and less prone to extraneous activities than say a bridge builder.

Organizational energy is part of this personality. It's generally measured by whether people in the organization are in a hurry or not, are tolerant or impatient with pending problems, or are comfortable or uncomfortable with the status quo and lack of movement.

Management expectations is another important component of organizational personality. It creates the work climate and tacitly sets the ground rules under which the various levels of management operate. Top management can, for example, expect that its people will exercise entrepreneurial initiative rather than hew to finely drawn policy limitations and well-defined procedures. It can be free wheeling, giving maximum opportunity for an executive to express his abilities, or it can be restrictive. Management says, "Look, this is your company, too. Work as though you're a partner. Get disturbed when you see a problem, and pitch in to solve it as fast as possible. If you have to set a precedent in the process, that's O.K. too." Or it can say, "You only work here, and we have our ways of doing things. They've been tried and tested, and they work to our satisfaction. Therefore, you will operate within the limits we've established."

In the extreme, the first attitude can create an uncoordinated hodgepodge, whereas the other can discourage all initiative and independent decision making. Although some time may be generally wasted with either extreme, the greater the tilt toward an entrepreneurial initiative environment, the faster the tempo and the more enthusiastic the participants. Whether top management controls this enthusiasm, shaping and using it to accomplish its goals, or is controlled by it markedly influences the organization's personality.

A fast-moving top management can create a basket full of new growth projects and fail at the same time to develop an organization large enough or competent enough to implement them. Projects can back up and stumble over each other. The organization can add frustration to its personality and a divisiveness can develop between top and lower levels of management, creating a nonproductive "we versus them" climate. Often top management will lash out in frustration, hiring and firing rapidly in an attempt to find the answer to an organizational deficiency. Lower levels become insecure, tending to act more defensively in their jobs. This obviously can slow tempo.

Varying levels of competence can affect an organization's personality. A fast-moving creative and innovative R&D department, for example, can run up against a ponderously moving marketing department. This can result in tempo-slowing conflict and frustration, as R&D sees its new hot ideas either shelved or handled ineptly.

Top managers can be nonlisteners, further exacerbating divisions. The can set fuzzy goals or poorly communicate good goals so no one knows what the hell the organization is really trying to do and what individual contributions are supposed to be. This adversely affects the organization's personality and slows the decision-making process. Or top managers can be motivators, sharply defining goals and inspiring the troops to contribute their best toward these goals. They can build pride in the organization, and this can speed up tempo.

Obviously, an organization's personality has more inputs and twists than we could possibly list here. The point is that tempo is a part of that personality, both influenced by it and markedly influencing it at the same time.

CHAPTER 5

Measuring Tempo— At Last, a Takeoff Point!

Another fable to illustrate another point:

A grizzled old weather-beaten Maine farmer is taking his ease, smoking his pipe and rocking on his porch, which faces a one-lane dirt road. Along comes (who else?) a city slicker, who screechingly brakes to a halt in front of the old farmer.

"Say, old timer," says the slicker. "Does this road go to Bangor?"

"Yep," says the farmer, missing not a beat on his rocker.

"Is it far?"

"Yep."

"Does this road widen out after a bit?"

"Yep."

"Can I get something to eat along here?"

"Nope."

"Thanks," says the slicker.

"Yep," nods the farmer.

Pretty soon the slicker staggers back down the road, sopping wet, clothes in shreds, bleeding here and there, an egg-size bump on his forehead.

"You crazy old man," he rails at the rocking farmer. "Why didn't you tell me the bridge was out over that cockamamy creek up the road?"

"You dern fool," replies the farmer with equal heat. "You didn't ask me."

Moral: Sometimes you can spot a problem by asking the right people the right questions. If you don't, you too can find yourself up the creek—or in it.

What we're going to do in this chapter is detail a method for getting a handle on an organization's present tempo for making and implementing decisions and relate this tempo to what it can or might be. And this, dear patient reader, is the takeoff point referred to earlier. Once we have established this takeoff point and know what we're dealing with, then we can take the next step of figuring out what to do to make a particular organization more decisive and faster paced.

We'll make no effort to evaluate this tempo in absolute terms—it can't be done—but rather to do so in relative terms of what it is versus what it can be. All this, of course, takes a good bit of subsurface information about the organization— for instance, how it works and how it perceives itself. What's the best source of this information? The executive team—the people closest to it, who both influence tempo the most and are influenced the most by it.

But asking an executive about his organization's tempo can create some problems of its own. Chances are he will answer both subjectively and defensively, seeing himself as a nonparticipant in the problem, merely its victim. His answer will depend on his frame of reference, which is generally how the other guys always move at a snail's pace and frustrate the hell out of the good guys, of which he of course is a most illustrious representative. But the fact is he can't address the subject from any useful perspective if he hasn't really thought about it in useful terms. (Philosophically, he'll agree that slow tempo exists, but we're after the "why.")

Finally, his answers will depend on a whole lot of other factors, such as his role as a decision maker in the organization, his relationship with his colleagues, his personal goals and ambitions, and his degree of frustration with getting his own recent ideas accepted or implemented.

With this in mind, the program for drawing out the information we'll need from the executive team is designed to work around these problems. This is done by questionnaire, but in no case is an executive asked to evaluate his own performance. The questions have been selected to uncover both the extent and the location of those barriers presently impeding a faster tempo. They are phrased in such a way as to elicit both specific and impressionistic answers, so that one can confirm the other. The questions are simply put, lending themselves to brief answers.

The questionnaire should be administered to people as part of a group. We'll call the process of questionnaire administration *testing* for want of a better word. The following steps are aimed at maximizing the effectiveness of the questionnaire.

1. Select an administrator of the test program, who will organize and conduct the testing and then evaluate its results. Where possible, to encourage maximum frankness, an outsider should be seriously considered. His role to those participating should be clearly explained: He is not there as a hit man, nor to evaluate personalities. His job is only to get answers, put them together, suggest where the organizational problem areas are, perhaps recommend some solutions, and then take off. If it's not feasible to use an outsider, then someone from within the organization with enough smarts to objectively understand the causes and nuances of slow decision making and to correlate the answers leading to useful conclusions could do it. This person should be pretty fast paced himself, so he can generate sympathetic enthusiasm. He should not be an intimidator, or be in a position to hire or fire respondents, or be responsible for their promotions or salary levels. He should enjoy their trust and respect. In short, his position and reputation should be such that the respondents

will be encouraged to answer the questions honestly, not to please the person asking them. The selection of a good administrator, from inside or out, is obviously the cornerstone of a successful test. We've listed his ideal qualifications. Doubtless most organizations will have to settle for something less. But if it's much less, the testing won't work.

2. Select as wide a cross-section of executives as possible from different levels of management and departments, but no more than 25 people. If the organization is large and divisions are well defined, enough different groups to cover a good segment within each division might be tested. A smaller company might want to include everybody, if that doesn't exceed 25. Ideally, the group should include both line and staff.

3. Explain the purpose of the program carefully to each person selected, stressing that he has been picked because he's in a position to make a significant contribution to the success of the project. He should be assured that, although his answers will be used as part of an overall analysis, they will *not* be seen by anyone else in the organization, except of course the test administrator, if he's part of the company. If any people exhibit reluctance or indicate they're not going to be wholly cooperative, it's best not to try to convince them otherwise. Scratch them, and select someone else.

4. A few days before the testing, give each participant a copy of the questionnaire so he can get the feel of it and have some time to think about what decisions he wants to use as examples. He should be cautioned not to attempt to answer any of the questions at this time. Chapters 3 and 4 of this book should be read for orientation *before* he looks over the questionnaire.

5. Select a meeting site: a boardroom or large conference room—or even better, for an environment designed to create more objectivity, a conference room at a local motel. An important point: To emphasize the *team* effort, seating should be at random and, where possible, all chairs, desks, and tables should be the same for everyone, with no distinction made

between the various levels of management. It should be stressed that, for the purposes of the test, the group consists of all Indians, no chiefs.

6. On D-day (early morning seems to be the best time), assemble the group and restate its purpose and mission. This next point is the second cornerstone of a successful test: The administrator should review with the group the material in Chapters 3 and 4. This overview should include the definition of tempo, its importance and relationship to slow decision making, and how it influences the activities of the whole company and its success or failure. The 11 elements of slow decision making should be reviewed and the participants' frames of reference oriented so they can relate their answers to these 11 elements. Without this background, the answers can wander all over the place and be neither useful, cohesive, nor relevant. It is crucial that the administrator know what he's talking about. If he doesn't, chances are none of the participants will take the project seriously. If he himself is familiar with Chapters 3 and 4, he'll probably be in pretty good shape.

7. Now the group should address the questionnaire and start writing.

8. At the completion of the written section, have the administrator generate a cross-table discussion. Anything that gets even close to personal accusation or recrimination should be called to a halt. Discussion of company policies, corporate procedures, and particularly organizational attitudes, however, not only are fair game but should in fact be encouraged. This discussion should not be rushed, nor should a deadline be imposed, since a world of information can be picked up at this point.

9. Depending on how this discussion goes, the administrator might give the participants a few more minutes to add to their written answers.

10. Then collect the answers. In addition to being a nice touch, the informality of a lunch following the test tends to

prolong an expression of viewpoints under relaxed conditions.

The questionnaire, with an introduction and review outline, appears on the following pages.

QUESTIONNAIRE

INTRODUCTION

You have been selected as part of this task force because we believe you can make a significant contribution to our goal of speeding up the pace of our organization. We want to be able to move a whole lot more quickly, to be lighter on our organizational feet. We want to make these fast-moving times work for us, not against us. We want to be out in front, not lagging behind.

Don't mistake this for a pie-in-the-sky, rally-round-the-flag idea. We're in deadly earnest. We've come to realize that the faster, more incisively we move, the more responsive we will be to problems and opportunities as they come along; that the quicker our organizational pulse beats, the more we can outdistance and out-gun our competition.

Obviously, to achieve this, we must know more about how our organization works—not in theory but in practice, not how we think it works or how we'd like it to work but how it moves and meshes every day in this very real world. We need to know more about our organization's strengths and weaknesses. This is why you have been selected—to help us find out.

You are specifically asked *not* to name individuals in any of your answers. We're not on a witch-hunt! You will be asked, however, to be specific as to departments or other segments of the organization and events. We simply need to know more about how we function as an organization—warts and all. This is why we ask you to be as frank and as objective as you can.

Rest assured that no one will see your answers except the person conducting this questionnaire. He'll weigh your answers and put them together with everyone else's to find a pattern. This pattern will tell us what we need to do organizationally to speed up our pace. If he feels that some of your ideas are so interesting that he'd like you to get credit for them, he'll ask your permission first before identifying you.

We thank you for your contribution to this very important organizational effort.

DEFINITION OF TEMPO

Organizational tempo is how fast an organization gets things done, makes decisions, implements them, reacts to changing business conditions and environments, identifies and solves problems, identifies and moves to grasp opportunities, reacts to competitors' moves, reacts to changing market conditions, and feeds back essential data. Tempo is the organization's pulse!

ELEMENTS THAT SLOW DECISION-MAKING TEMPO

1. Timidity
   Personal—fear of making a commitment that could result in a mistake or change an otherwise comfortable status quo.
   Organizational—fear induced by the view that *every* mistake is judged as a bad performance rather than considered a basis for learning.
2. Incompetence
   Decision maker's inability to solve a problem or to take advantage of an opportunity. Lack of experience might have similar results.
3. Vague decision-making responsibility

Uncertainty about who is charged with a particular responsibility or who will make a particular decision and
also be able to make it stick.

4. Decision drift
Lack of a firm target date by which a decision must be
made to maximize its effectiveness. Decision drift is the
difference between the time necessary to make a decision and the time it actually takes for the decision to get
made.

5. Remoteness of decision maker from problem or opportunity
Results in a lack of the sense of urgency that someone
closer to it might feel, or prevents a full appreciation of
nuances and ramifications.

6. Loss of decision-making momentum
Too many people involved either as contributors or as po-
tential decision stoppers.
Too many inconclusive, unproductive meetings.

7. Improper delegation
No delegation at all.
Nominal delegation, but too much control retained by
delegator over methods and procedures.
Delegation to the wrong people, improper training of sub-
ordinates, or poor guidance and follow-up by delegator.

8. Lack of authority to fully control elements of decision
Lack of cooperation, in terms of time or content, by those
whose inputs are sought.

9. Corporate politics and factionalism
Competing goals and competition for influence, leading to
conflict and lack of support for decision maker's efforts
to make decisions.

10. Long lead time between decision and implementation
Loss of initial enthusiasm, of sense of urgency, and of incentive to make fast or innovative decisions about implementation.

11. Organizational personality

Management expectations, sometimes discouraging entrepreneurial spirit and establishing overly confining procedures.

Poor definition or communication of goals and of what
contributions are expected from individuals to achieve
these goals.

Note: Please keep your answers as brief as possible. In some
cases, two or three words or a simple "yes" or "no" will suffice.
However, don't be afraid to elaborate if you have a point or
observation you think bears more explanation.

Section 1

The following list of questions is designed to give us an overview
of where and why pockets of slow decision making exist in our
organization. That they exist, we all know, because they exist in
every organization to some extent. Remember, it's the "why"
we're really plumbing for.

So we'll ask you to zero in on one department, on part of one,
or on some other segment of our organization that you consider
to be slow tempoed. We're not looking for proof, merely your
impressions and opinions.

On the left-hand side, indicate the department or organizational segment and use the following check system:

√   "Not really a problem"
√√   "Often a problem"
√√√ "A major problem"

Then on the right-hand side, use the same check system for the
company as a whole. This doesn't necessarily mean that every

facet of the company conforms to your evaluation but that the problem areas you check are sufficiently widespread that we ought to be aware of them.

(a) In general, is decision making slowed because of personal timidity; that is, does the decision maker tend to be reluctant to make decisions because of a fear of making a mistake or of upsetting an apple cart?

(b) Is there often a reluctance to make decisions because of frequent unpleasant conflict with others, perhaps even within the same department, who hold opposite views?

(c) Is there often a reluctance to make decisions because of a feeling of futility on the part of some decision makers, especially at lower levels of management, who sense their decisions or ideas will be ignored or rejected regardless of merit?

(d) Does the department tend at some or all levels to lack the motivation to do something about problems because each mistake is judged critically rather than viewed in a more supportive manner? "Hey, nice try. Bad result. At least we did something. Now let's make another decision quickly to correct the goof and hope we've learned from it so we don't do it again."

(e) Is there frequently confusion about who is really responsible for making the decision once a problem or opportunity is brought into focus?

(f) Or do we know who is *supposed* to decide, but does the person charged with making certain decisions keep sidestepping so when the matter comes up we don't really know where to bring it for decision?

(g) When problems or opportunities are brought up, does the decision-making process tend to get started without a time limit being set? Is there a shoulder-shrugging rationale of "well, hell, these things take time," resulting in a lack of urgency to make decisions as fast as possible so problems can be corrected quickly?

(h) Is decision making often slowed because the final decision makers are too far away from the problem or the opportunity and lack the sense of urgency to do something quickly that those closest to it would have?

(i) Is the atmosphere among departments and individual executives fairly cooperative, so that an executive can count on getting input when *he* thinks he needs it, not when the other person gets around to it? In other words, are our goals and objectives so clearly defined and understood that respect is shown for the other fellow's priorities?

(j) To follow up on the last question: Are we so coordinated that, if a decision cuts across departmental lines and inputs are required from each department, the machinery and the coordinator are firmly in place and functioning so that information and decision flows smoothly, or do our various departments tend to operate in isolation?

(k) Do certain decisions have to climb the chain of command, involving so many people that they often get delayed and sometimes lost because either the machinery to track them properly doesn't work or the people who asked for the decision simply don't have enough clout, incentive, or forcefulness to jar them loose?

(l) Is the department's decision making slowed because it doesn't delegate enough? In other words, are too few people holding too many reins, especially on routine operating matters that could easily be passed on to someone else who could and would make the decisions faster?

(m) Are many decisions made pretty quickly and then bottled up and delayed when they go to someone else for approval? In short, is our approval process significantly slowing up the total decision-making process, perhaps even discouraging the making of fast decisions at lower levels?

(n) Is lack of competence a problem? (Be careful not to let your prejudices intrude here. Because someone doesn't agree with you doesn't necessarily mean he's wrong and you're right or that you see the whole picture.) Do decisions often get hung up because some decision makers simply aren't too sure of how to handle the problem or the opportunity?

(o) To follow up on the last question: No one knows everything. If the decision maker isn't sure what to do, does he admit it freely and seek help from others so he can move ahead with making the decision?

(p) Once a decision is made, do people have a sense of urgency about starting to implement it right quick? Or are we pretty fast on the draw with making decisions and do we then let implementation drag out the whole process so the decisions themselves have little effect?

(q) When a decision is made, is there a tendency to schedule implementation at the *same time?*

(r) So much for the slow-tempoed segments of the organization. Now switch gears. Name one that you consider to be fast tempoed. List very briefly a few key elements that you think contribute to this fast pace. Test it against these sample questions:

Does its leadership set a good example?

Does its leadership demand a fast pace?

Are its people always working on so many new projects that they simply don't have the time to get bogged down?

Is the segment, by and large, deadline conscious?

Do the people seem to move ahead at a good clip, not fretting too much about what they're leaving behind?

Does leadership delegate pretty freely, giving most subordinates a feeling of active participation?

(s) How would you rate the morale of this fast-tempoed department?

(Check one: High   Fair   Poor)

How would you rate the morale of the slow-tempoed one?

(Check one: High   Fair   Poor)

Section 2

Select a recent decision that took a month or more between the time the subject first came up and the time the decision was finally made. If you were close to or involved in the decision and know its gestation pains fairly intimately, so much the better.

This could have been a decision to do something—or *not* to do something. It could be in the area of opening new facilities (or closing them), developing new products, changing product materials, getting prices, dealing with labor problems, creating new marketing programs, solving a production personnel problem, reacting to something a competitor did that hurt us (or something we did that hurt him), making a significant equipment purchase, or reorganizing some facet of our business—in short, anything that might have had a significant impact on the company.

What was the subject matter or problem?

Very briefly, what was decided?

Approximately how long did it take to make the decision once the problem or opportunity was first identified?

Now—take this next part literally: *Assume that the very life of the company depended on that decision having been made in half the time it actually took! Assume everything would go—the company, your job, everything!*

How about it? Could we have made the decision in half the time?

As you look back, can you pinpoint those factors that in your opinion prevented the decision from having been made in less time? What were they? Can you estimate in general terms what each cost us in time? That is, was it days, weeks, or months?

To have made the decision in half the time, would we have had to have ridden roughshod over any red tape or corporate procedures?

To close some of these gaps, could we have speeded up data input? What informational inputs, if any, would we have had to forgo? In the final analysis would we have missed them? Was there an attempt to amass so much information in the hope of making a "riskless" decision that the time factor paid for it?

Was the decision making encumbered by a succession of

meetings? Did it take a long time in between to assemble the meeting groups? Were some or many of these meetings inconclusive, and did they have to be followed up by other meetings as a result? Could the subject matter of these meetings (or some of them) have been handled by one or two people acting alone?

Did the person who was supposed to make the decision delay it by simply sitting on it or letting time pass for no obvious reason? (Bear in mind, he could have had a reason you weren't aware of.) Or was there an obvious reason? If so, what? (Might be a good time to refer again to the summary of elements of slow decision making.)

Did the decision maker get cooperation from others?

Did the decision maker fail to push others who had to contribute to the decision, or did he simply let the process develop its own momentum?

Was the decision slowed at the approval levels? Did too many people have to approve?

In your opinion, was the pace of this decision fairly typical for the department or organizational segment? Is it typical of many departments or organizational segments throughout the company? Is it typical of our overall pace?

If we had made a decision in half the time, do you think it would have been different from the one we actually made?

If we had made it in half the time, what benefit, if any, would we have derived from doing so—for example, solving the problem quicker and reducing the cost drain?

Very briefly, list two or three steps you would have taken if it had been your responsibility to make this decision in half the time it actually took.

Section 3

Now let's take a look at a decision that we implemented, a decision that had some noticeable impact on the company. Select one that you think could have been implemented faster than it was. For example, suppose we decided to rearrange a production line or make a change in one of our products, how long did it take before we really got our teeth into doing it?

What was the decision?

After it was made, how long did it take before implementation got into high gear? (Check one: Days   Weeks   Months)

Now again, *assume that the very life of our company depended on that decision having been implemented in half the time it actually took!*

Could we have done it if we really had to?

In order to implement most decisions, it's necessary to make many other decisions. For example, if we decided to enlarge our R&D facilities, we would have to decide on such things as a contractor, purchase orders for new equipment, and where to find additional staff. Were we slow in making such decisions? Can you name one or more? How long did they take to make, and, in your opinion, how long should they have taken? What effect did they have in slowing down the implementation of the decision? (Check one: Days   Weeks   Months)

Any idea why they took so long? Did somebody "just not get to it"? Was somebody waiting for information that someone else held up? If so, was there a big push to get it? Did other projects or crises arise that took time away from addressing this project?

Did any red tape, corporate procedures, excessive meetings, and the like hold up the implementation process? How about approvals for implemention decisions? Did they hold up the project?

Did we approach the project with a sense of urgency, or did we just let it fall into place as we went along? What was the attitude of those involved? Did we react somewhat passively when some element of it bogged down, or did we make an intensive effort to find the most innovative, fastest, most direct path to get it done?

In your opinion, were the components of the implementation

process improperly delegated? In other words, if someone who was pretty busy had said to someone else, "Here, you do it and keep me posted," would this have speeded up the process?

Now again, suppose the survival of the company depended on our having implemented the decision in half the time it actually took, and suppose you had been given complete authority and responsibility. List one or two changes in approach you would have made (for example, setting or tightening deadlines for the various phases of the project).

Would your way have been any more costly than the way it was done (a lot of overtime, for example)? If we had implemented the decisions faster, what benefits, besides freeing up more time for other projects, would we have derived from having the project functioning sooner?

In your opinion, was the pace of implementing this decision typical of the way most decisions are implemented throughout the company or a large part of it?

Section 4

Now let's take a look at decision drift. This, as you will remember, is when a decision that should require only a few serious hours' input takes months to make. No one is quite sure why. It "just happens."

List two decisions that are now "drifting," matters brought up some time ago for which no firm decision has yet been made.

Roughly how long ago were these first brought up? To put it another way, approximately when was the problem or opportunity first recognized and verbalized and when did someone first say, "O.K., let's do something about it"?

In your opinion, are we being hurt by the delay? Is there a problem now kicking around unsolved, perhaps getting progressively worse? Are we missing or did we miss an opportunity? Are other projects waiting for this one to get into place first?

If the person in charge is just too busy to make decisions and the authority has been delegated to someone else, would the decisions get made? Competently?

Generally, do we as an organization tend to make many of our decisions when impelled to by crises, or do we make decisions before the crises hit?

Think this one out carefully: In your opinion, could the two pending decisions you listed be made within 24 hours from right now if someone really *had* to?

In your opinion, how serious is our decision drift problem overall? (Check one: Very   Not very   Enough so we should be concerned about it)

Section 5

Let's take a hypothetical situation: One of our buyers is approached by a salesman selling a new piece of equipment that he claims will reduce our manufacturing costs by a goodly percentage. Chances are our buyer will contact someone in engineering or manufacturing. Certain evaluations will have to be made and perhaps verified: cost projections, pay-back period estimates, space considerations, budgets, approvals, and the like. Say the equipment costs $100,000, and we finally determine that it will cut our manufacturing costs by a percentage sufficient to result in a pay-back period of one year. We decide to go with it.

With your knowledge of how fast we move, the number of people that must get involved, our procedures for handling such a project, the meetings we must schedule, and so on, what is your best guess (and we realize that at best it's only an educated guess) as to how long it would take from the time our buyer is first approached by the equipment salesman until our purchase order is finally written? (Check one: 1 week   1 month 2–3 months   4–6 months   Over 6 months)

If you checked "2–3 months" or longer, run down the summary of elements of slow decision making and list, by numbers only, those elements you think might work to prevent the purchase order from being written in less time.

If you checked "2–3 months" or longer, answer this: Suppose an "or else" directive came down from on high that the decision *had* to be made within one month or less. What would we have to do? Would it simply be a matter of everyone concerned moving faster, perhaps making faster judgments and decisions, or are there procedural problems standing in the way (the number of people that must get involved, the number of meetings that must be held, perhaps the number of people who share the responsibility for making the decision)? Spell it out.

List the various departments and segments of departments that would have to get involved in such a decision. Check the one you think might hold it up the longest beyond what is necessary. Is it because the department is particularly busy, or is its normal pace too slow?

Section 6

Finally, let's get some of your general perceptions.
   (a) How would you describe our organization? (Check one: Fast moving overall   Fast moving with occasional slow-moving pockets   Overall, slow moving and cumbersome)
   (b) How would you rate our general level of enthusiasm? (Check one: High   Low   Somewhere in between)
   (c) In general, are we constantly being "stretched" by new challenges, or do we tend to get into a mechanical routine and react to new projects as interruptions rather than opportunities?
   (d) As a rule, do our meetings tend to be long, redundant, and inconclusive? Or do we usually seem impatient to finish our

business and get back to work? Do we too readily schedule additional meetings to deal with business we could have settled in a previous meeting?

(e) Do you feel that many people in our organization are discouraged from thinking creatively about our problems and opportunities because the climate for getting decisions on their ideas is too slow or unresponsive? If so, how would you rate the problem? (Check one: Very serious   Not serious   Serious enough to be of concern)

(f) Do you feel that we're all pulling together, that top management is giving the organization a firm direction (yes or no) with clear-cut goals (yes or no) and is doing a good job of communicating these goals (yes or no) as well as clearly defining the individual contributions needed to achieve these goals (yes or no)? (Feel free to expand on this question with a few comments if you think you can pinpoint some of the problem areas. If you have a suggestion or two, put them down—but be brief!)

(g) Do you think suppliers, customers, and competitors view us as fast or slow paced, aggressive or passive, decisive or nondecisive? Do you think these perceptions are justified?

(h) Do you think most of us feel we're a team out to show the rest of the world that we're pretty damn good at what we do? Or do most of us feel we're just a group of individuals loping along simply earning our daily bread?

(i) Is our attitude and decision-making process geared to listening to the problems and suggestions of our labor force, or have we tuned them out? If we've tuned them out, how would you rate the problem? (Check one: Serious   Moderately serious   Not serious)

(j) In your opinion, if we do have a tempo problem, at what levels of management is it most pronounced? (Check as many as you think apply. Double-check the level you think is the worst. Top   Top-middle   Middle   Lower).

(k) O.K., now you've given us an idea of what we're doing

wrong. Thanks. Now take a few minutes and list what you think are some of our strong points. Tell us what departments, in your opinion, are doing a bang-up job. Tell us what attitudes we've got that are good strong bases upon which to build. In short, tell us where as an organization we're doing a good job. We promise not to blush.

CHAPTER 6

Now That We Have the Takeoff Point . . .

Another story, another point:

Charlie Chan, world-famous detective, was called into a murder case. These were the facts: There were two men in a locked room, one dead. The second man was found standing over the dead man, holding a smoking pistol. A knife twixt the departed's shoulder blades bore the fingerprints of the second man. As the police broke into the room, they heard the second man say, "I shot him. I stabbed him!"

"What do you think, Charlie?" asked the police lieutenant as they surveyed the scene.

"Ah," said the inscrutable Mr. Chan. " 'Facts' designed to look like man with gun killed dead man. But must look behind 'facts' for truth. Dead man's wife asked supposed murderer to cut loaf of bread in kitchen for corned beef on rye, light on mustard. Wife then stuck knife in husband's back, careful not to disturb suspect's fingerprints. Wearing gloves, wife next shot husband, called in suspect from kitchen, handed him gun, and said, 'Hold gun. Must go to supermarket. Be back soon.' Wife then locked door from outside, took key, and called police. When police break down door, one said, 'Aha, you fiend! You shot and stabbed dead man!' Suspect merely said with disbelief, 'I shot him? I stabbed him?' So, regret to say, wife is murderer and suspect is poor slob."

The lieutenant thought this over. "Sorry, Charlie," he said finally. "The dead guy didn't have a wife."

"Ah so," said Charlie. "Win some, lose some. What in hell. Old Charlie gave it good shot. Next time this humble detective not ignore obvious."

Moral: If you overlook the obvious, you may end up with an organization that gets away with murder.

The point of this story is, of course, that in most cases the pattern of test answers will give us some pretty obvious clues as to where and what is wrong with the organization. For example, if a number of negative comments are made about a segment of an organization in the first five sections, it's a pretty good clue that that segment contributes to slow tempo. In most cases, the causes will also show up in a pattern. The differences between the time it took to make or implement a decision and the time respondents think it could have taken if there was real pressure to act quickly can provide a guide to the severity of the problem, as can the length of time a decision has been in drift (Section 4) and the level of morale in the organization (Section 6). In most cases, analyses will be this simple.

However, in deference to old Charlie's philosophy of looking for the truth behind the "facts," it must be admitted that sometimes a successful analysis involves some art along with the science of collating numbers and can uncover some causes not wholly obvious from the test responses. The administrator, therefore, should not hesitate to follow up his paperwork analysis with as many individual post-test interviews as are necessary to clarify and elaborate some of the views expressed in the questionnaire responses.

With this in mind, let's take a look at three cases where the causes of the problem turned out to be different from the obvious conclusions one would normally draw from the test responses. While each case actually involved many trends and indicators, we'll highlight only some of these for purposes of illustration. (Incidentally, the organizations referred to in this chapter, as throughout this book, are sufficiently masked so that even old Charlie couldn't identify them).

CASE 1

Jones Equipment Co. Valve manufacturer. Midwest. 850 employees. Sales, approximately $93 million. Two plants in two different industrial parks. Offices and corporate staff in downtown office building, 6 miles from one plant, 38 miles from the second. One plant and corporate staff tested together, 18 executives out of approximately 57. Special note: Engineering department was part of corporate staff, under a VP whose primary function was to assist plants with engineering problems, generally on a request basis. Company growth, approximately 6 percent (sales) per year average past four years versus 11 percent industry average.

Test Results

Section 1. Nine respondents, including two from engineering, picked engineering as their slow-tempoed example. Eight picked timidity as a cause, a pretty significant figure. Six checked fuzzy responsibility. Five indicated a problem with cooperation among the department's managers. In most cases, responses were multiple checks, indicating a "major problem." At the end of Section 1, one could sense chaos in the engineering department.

    Section 2. Eight used a dragged-out decision that involved engineering. Their reasons supported their responses to Section 1.

Section 3 continued the trend. Nine respondents selected a decision that involved the engineering department as an example of a decision that was slow to be implemented.

Section 4. Nine selected decisions that involved the engineering department as examples of decision drift.

Section 5. Eleven had a field day in criticizing the engineering department. All eleven indicated, some quite strongly, that the department would be the major stumbling block to getting the equipment purchased in a hurry.

Section 6 picked up a pretty good consensus that the company as a whole was being held back by a few pockets (read "engineering department," primarily) in its ability to get things done.

Analysis

This was one of the cases where the test answers seemed to leave little room for doubt. As constituted, the engineering department was a loser. The post-test discussion painted a pretty clear, although cautiously stated, picture of the department being the subject of considerable water-cooler conversation and frustration among several groups of executives, especially, as would be expected, production management.

In the same vein, the primary cause seemed to revolve around the matter of leadership, and further follow-up investigation revealed that indeed it was. The VP of engineering was getting along in years, and seemed to be growing more conservative and cautious with age. It reached the point where he spent more time avoiding risks than in getting things done. He apparently wanted to hold on to the reins pretty tightly, not merely to guide and direct with a strong hand, but rather to play the role of company protector. This was understandable. He had been with the company since its founding, was somewhat responsible for its success, and was personally close to the chairman-founder. As a result he had been fairly well insulated from overt criticism, until the test revealed the problem.

What to Do

The obvious solution appeared to be to give the VP a kick upstairs or early retirement and replace him with someone better equipped to organize and tighten up the department's performance. But the test answers picked up another problem: Engineering was viewed as a staff function instead of a line function. Management's unquestioned philosophy had been, "Let the plants worry only about turning gears. We'll give them all the support they need from headquarters. This way we can control and coordinate the two plants and do it with one general and administrative overhead instead of two."

However, the replies to several questions suggested that, in addition to having ragged leadership, the engineering department was simply located in the wrong place. Four respondents from plant and production indicated that a major problem was not only lack of coordination but also lack of communication between production management and engineering. A perceptive buyer from the purchasing department (corporate) also noted this gap in Section 2 and asked rhetorically, "What engineering problems are there *downtown?*" It appeared that the remoteness of the department from where the problems it was supposed to solve were and its leadership under a *corporate* VP created a nonnavigable chasm. With this fact brought sharply into focus by the questionnaire, the decision was made to break up the department and reassign its functions and personnel to the two plants. The department was now brought snug up to the engineering problems in the plants, and its efforts were coordinated and directed by plant management.

The gap was closed, and the barrier to faster decision making crumbled.

P.S. Having lost his power base, the VP retired.

CASE 2

Smith Industries. Electronics manufacturer (computer components). Headquartered East Coast. 1,600 employees. Sales: $158 million. Six plants, five of which came about as a result of acquisitions. Executives from two plants tested together with corporate staff, 22 out of a possible 112 executives. Special note: Management is aware that competition is outscoring it in new product development and profit margins.

Test Results

Section 1. A wide cross-section of organizational segments were selected as examples of slow tempo, especially plant management, R&D, engineering, marketing, and purchasing. Oddly enough, timidity did not score as high as would be expected. However, reluctance to make decisions because of futility and not knowing who was really responsible for making decisions scored high with lower-level executives. Lack of decision time limits and absence of feelings of urgency also scored high. Remote decision makers and too much chain-of-command involvement were also frequently cited as causes of slow tempo, especially by middle managers. Delegation also got clobbered and with it the company's decision-approval process. Competence did not appear to be a problem. Only two departments scored well in being fast tempoed, personnel and product field service. (It looked as though the respondents were hard put to come up with examples.) Significantly, six executives did not give any examples of fast-tempoed departments, suggesting that the problem was systemic.

Section 2. Fourteen respondents zeroed in on corporate procedures as a major problem. The procedure identified in nine answers was the approval process. Eleven respondents felt decisions tended to be slowed by an overaccumulation of unnecessary data (indicating a high level of defensive decision making). Twelve indicated meetings slowed decision making. Thirteen replies suggested that shortcutting the approval process would make faster decisions possible.

Section 3. The question of slow implementation picked up again on the theme of slow decision making and revealed much the same pattern established by Sections 1 and 2, especially as it related to the approval process.

Section 4. Decision drift was considered by most as a major problem. Fourteen respondents thought it could have been corrected by better delegation. Thirteen believed decisions got made only when the problems they were to solve became crises.

Section 5. Again, the hypothetical situation pointed to a general decision-making malaise, with approval authorities taking the lumps.

Section 6. The organization as a whole scored low on tempo and enthusiasm. Only 6 out of the 22 respondents indicated they felt any excitement in the air over the pace of movement. The questions about whether top management was giving the organization a "firm direction" with "clear-cut goals" and doing a "good job of communicating these goals" were each answered with a pretty resounding "no." Nine double checked top management as the slowest-moving level of management.

Interestingly, one of the top three executives took the test. His answers ran completely counter to the consensus. If there was a problem, he didn't see it in the same light as everyone else. A significant point.

Analysis

Approval procedures were the *problem*. The *cause* soon became apparent and tied into an element noted in the brief description of the company: Five of the six plants came about as a result of acquisitions. Top management was weak and unsure when it came to operations. Its group forte was wheeling and dealing financially. While acquiring plants by merger and intricate financing, it also acquired new products, sales, and profits. When there was a pause in the acquisition program, few new products were developed, because internal product development was minimal; sales softened and profits slipped.

The financially oriented troika involved itself in virtually every decision as an approval authority. Any expenditure over $3,000 had to be approved by the president, and anything over $15,000 by the executive finance committee (the three top executives). It was obvious that they had a problem fully appreciating the nature and potential of proposed new products. While two of them had some engineering background, they were too many years behind the technological advances in the industry to fully appreciate their significance. But they were pretty good at reading dollar signs, and any potential expenditure was perceived as a possible "risk of hard-earned money." Suggestions for updating equipment and manufacturing techniques inevitably engendered wariness: "Are you sure it'll pay for itself in [x] months?" Any expression of even a minor doubt in response to the question was the kiss of death for the idea. While most decisions dragged out at this approval stage, many simply drifted into oblivion. Decision stagnation filtered downward through the whole organization (which was why so many segments were named as slow tempoed in Section 1). In frustration, many competent executives had sought more fertile fields elsewhere. All the trend lines now pointed toward eventual disaster.

What to Do

While the analysis clearly pointed up a ponderous process for approving decisions at top-management levels, the problem appeared to go deeper. It was not only the process but top management itself. As a result, three basic steps were outlined for action. With some initial reluctance, top management accepted the fact that its strength was in financial wheeling and dealing and acquisitions, *not* operations. With even more reluctance, the troika removed itself somewhat from the decision-making process. This was done by simply raising significantly the amount of money managers at various levels could spend without presidential or executive finance committee approval. Second, shortly thereafter, a very effective executive VP was hired to pump in some outside perspective. Under his leadership, the operating levels were reoriented for more incisive decision making by formalizing delegation (top management to top-middle and middle), more precisely defining and enlarging scopes of responsibilities, and establishing time limits for decisions in certain critical areas. The third step was simply to start restaffing the organization with new R&D and marketing people to replace those who had quit in frustration and to reemphasize these two pathfinder departments.

The top managers (the three founders) now geared themselves to spend more time on acquisitions and less on budget reviews. (Actually, their acquisitions amounted to one small one in the following year. Their time on the golf course filled the gap very nicely. No one complained.) Whereas they had previously reviewed budgets on a monthly basis, they now reviewed them quarterly. This was designed to give operating people more freedom to get longer range plans in place and under way without having to defend them at every step. Within seven months after top management discovered that its world wasn't falling apart as it delegated many of its responsibilities, the executive VP began to handle the quarterly reviews and budget planning, and top management was involved only on a 6-month, after-the-fact review basis. Admittedly, this was not a "book" solution. Top management in a very real sense was encouraged to abdicate many of the fiscal responsibilities reserved for top management. In practice, however, the solution was tailored to the company, its people, its rather deep-set attitudes and philosophies, its strengths and its weaknesses (most of which were brought into focus by the test, and all of which needed a highly individualized fundamental change to get the company back on course).

CASE 3

Brown Manufacturing Co. Luggage manufacturer. Located in Northeast. One luggage manufacturing plant; one plastics plant providing some materials for the former. 800 employees. Sales: $65 million range. Seventeen executives from luggage manufacturing plant tested, out of possible 39. Special note: Top management saw profit margins shrinking on a rising sales curve and concluded that the company wasn't responding quickly enough to counter rising costs.

Test Results

Section 1 indicated slow-tempoed areas in purchasing, engineering, marketing, shipping, and plant administration. Ten respondents, a significant number, believed a problem existed because no one knew who was really responsible for what. Eleven indicated they thought decision making got started without any target dates. Nine people felt that there was a lack of cooperation between executive groups and that little respect was shown for other people's priorities. Ten people suggested a lack of interdepartmental cooperation.

In Section 2, respondents mentioned 12 different decisions. Significantly, 11 people pinpointed meetings as encumbering decision making.

In Section 3, meetings again cropped up as a problem in getting implementation under way quickly. Ten respondents suggested that they could have speeded up the decision making and implementation by reducing the number of people who had to get involved and concentrating decision-making responsibility in fewer hands.

In Section 4, the 17 respondents noted 12 examples of decision drift, which pretty much attested to the widespread nature of the problem. Most indicated that decision drift was too often a serious problem. The large number of people that had to get involved in a decision was blamed by 11 respondents.

Section 5 was a key question in view of the objective of the company—to find out why it wasn't responding quickly enough in countering rising costs. The average length of time it would take to purchase the cost-saving equipment was predicted as four to six months! The reason, according to 13 respondents, was again the number of people and meetings that would have to be involved.

In Section 6, the question about meetings continued the trend. Twleve respondents said, "Yes, our meetings are too long, redundant, and inconclusive."

Analysis

One thread ran through the test replies: Things weren't getting done because of the number of people and the number of meetings involved in the process of trying to get something decided. That much was obvious. In view of how obvious this was to everyone else, why then hadn't top management spotted it? The fact is top management was well aware of it, but it told itself the problem was not the system but rather how to make the system work.

Management prided itself on its "enlightened" approach to decision making. "We recognize that everything any one organizational segment does has an effect on every other segment and on the company as a whole. Because no department operates in a vacuum, our philosophy is to give each a chance to input. The validity of this approach is attested to by our record for *not* making bloopers, which is pretty damn good." True, except that its record for getting changes made was *not* pretty damn good. In fact, it wasn't doing much at all except meeting in committees. It's pretty hard to make a blooper when it takes "four to six months" (which might have been a slight exaggeration, but not much) to make a decision that could and should be made in a matter of weeks. The real blooper was of course the time factor, but management failed to recognize this as a blooper. So costs rose at a rapid rate because of inflation, while decisions to increase efficiency to offset the cost increases that couldn't be offset by higher pricing piddled along at a much slower rate. It doesn't take someone with a whole lot of smarts to predict the results of these rate differentials.

To buy a new piece of equipment required inputs from purchasing, product engineering, industrial engineering, production management, product management, quality control, and, finally, cost accounting. As though this wasn't bad enough, several of the input groups were committees of two or more people. And each group head had to "sign off" as approving the purchase. The system, designed to be thorough and to minimize risks, was considered by management, according to one VP, as "a hell of a good example of the application of participative management." But it simply fell apart so far as its ability to make timely decisions was concerned.

What to Do

The twin principles of widespread interdepartmental input and participative management were the focus of the company's management philosophy. The test results spotlighted the obvious contradiction of philosophy and results. So the company switched gears, not without some anguish. The sign-off procedures were abandoned, and each segment no longer had to be completely satisfied before a decision was made. Decision-making authority was streamlined so that, for example, in the case of most new pieces of manufacturing equipment, the plant manager made the decision. It was up to him to get recommendations from everyone else concerned and to filter out those recommendations he considered pertinent and useful. The plant manager could override objections and stick by his decision, subject to approval by a VP if the amount to be spent was over $10,000 and under $50,000. Purchases above $50,000 required the approval of the president. Below $10,000, the plant manager was on his own.

The company's management focus now shifted from thoroughness and participative management to more individual responsibility—a structure better suited for faster decision making and one more responsive to the company's real need of keeping its cost reduction program in step with the pressures of outside cost increases.

A SPECIAL NOTE

A very significant element surfaces in these three cases, one that is supported in many other cases not covered here. In theory, this element is painfully obvious; in practice, it is very difficult to identify and change. What top management considers organizational "virtues" often turn out to be organizational "vices" when their *application* is put into perspective. When changes to improve organizational effectiveness are considered, these "virtues" (actually certain principles of management that management is high on) are viewed as sacrosanct and untouchable. After all, when trying to make something better, you don't tamper with what's right. You go after what's wrong.

The problem is of course that every organization is unique in character, personality, work habits, philosophies, background, perceptions, leadership, market position, and so on. So what is right for one may be dead wrong for another. When we blindly accept a principle that's valid for a large percentage of *other* organizations, we tend not to question it, its application, or its real effect on us.

For example, the principle of corporate staff support for a multiplant organization is fine and workable in a large percentage of organizations. But in the case of Jones Equipment (Case 1), it didn't work with the engineering department, because Jones's situation was different. The department had developed its own peculiar relationship with the operating plants. For a variety of reasons, this relationship produced a low level of expectations of the service the plants would receive. In time, the plants accommodated to this, and having a number of unresolved problems was accepted as a fact of company life. Because the basic principle of corporate staff support was accepted and nurtured, no one thought to question how well it worked at Jones's until the tempo test coordinated and focused the opposition.

But is this a typical experience? Well, let's look at Smith Industries (Case 2), which had a similar problem, only its "virtue" was the exercise of tight fiscal controls by its top management. It's pretty hard to quarrel with the principle that any company that fails to maintain a tight fiscal control is heading hell-bent for disaster. Yet Smith's blind acceptance of the principle obscured its own peculiar application of it. When sales and profits slipped, top management, with its weak background in operations, simply tightened fiscal control on the theory that if tight is good, tighter is better. In this case, tighter was leading to strangulation and exacerbating the very thing it was trying to correct. When the tempo test indicated that the organization was gasping for breath, controls were loosened and responsibility redirected.

At Brown Manufacturing (Case 3), the phrases "participative management." "no department operates in a vacuum," "get input from every department involved and keep our percentage of bloopers to practically zilch" were frequently heard. Valid principles? Of course. Yet Brown, because it took so long to make decisions, was on the road to self-destruction, until the tempo test provided an overview of Brown's own peculiar situation.

ONE CAVEAT

None of the above suggests that we should throw out a management's cherished principles as a matter of course when something goes awry. The principles may be valid, but the application wrong or inept. It may be a matter of personnel, follow-up, support, or the type of management leadership that needs to be addressed. I used these three cases not only to show how a tempo test can uncover the tempo-slowing areas and their causes but also to illustrate what happens when a company fails, attempting at the same time to examine its organizational sacred cows and to emphasize that each organization has its own individual characteristics that call for its own solutions to its own peculiar problems. This, incidentally, also illustrates the hazards of universally applying academic generalizations in seeking solutions to organizational problems.

CHAPTER 7

Management by Decisions— One Road to Faster Tempo

A true story:

The customer service department of a computer manufacturing company received several complaints from the field service force that a printed circuit (PC) board was loosening up in shipment. The head of the department fired off a memo to the head of product engineering, who promptly assigned an engineer to look into it. At the same time, he gave the engineer a second assignment: to evaluate and supervise some durability tests on a new plastic cover. These tests were to be coordinated with the cover's manufacturer. The manufacturer's salesman was a heavy-handed entertainer, and somehow, between martini lunches and a few martini-laced dinners, the engineer got the idea that maybe the possibility of saving $4.37 per cover was a hell of a lot more important than a few PC boards loosening up.

Meanwhile, one of the computer company's salesmen visited a customer he thought was ready for more CRT units. "Your terminals are giving us a fit," he was told. "Your field service people are in and out of here like a revolving door tightening up PC boards. If you can't ship workable units, maybe we'd better look somewhere else."

The salesman called his sales manager who a week later (don't ask why it took a week) called the traffic department.

"What's happening to our CRT units? Can't you guys ship them out without busting up PC boards?"

The head of traffic called the head of product engineering. "Hear about our PC boards popping loose?" "Sure," was the reply, "we're working on it."

The sales manager received some more complaints. He called traffic again. "What the hell is happening? What's being done about the loose PC boards?" "No sweat," he was told. "Product engineering is working on the problem."

The head of traffic thought maybe he'd better play it safe. He called the head of product engineering. "You guys *are* working on the problem, aren't you?" he asked. "Of course," was the reply.

The head of product engineering called in the engineer he had assigned to the problem. "What's with those loose PC boards?" he asked. "It's a shipping problem," the engineer replied flatly. "They need a better package."

The head of product engineering called the head of traffic. "It's your problem. The product's O.K. Try a better package."

The head of traffic called in the head of package engineering. "You solve the problem. Our package isn't working," he told him.

The head of package engineering called in a host of packaging manufacturers. "Whoever solves the problem at an *economical* cost gets to make the package for us," he told them.

The race was on. Packages were designed, tested, and failed. On a discordant note, two of the packaging manufacturers told the head of package engineering that the problem was not the packaging but the way the PC boards were anchored to the chassis. They were not invited back. End of discord.

By this time, approximately four and a half months had passed since the first complaint. During this period, 4,200 CRTs had been shipped, with 362 complaints received about loose PC boards. Cost to service these complaint: $62,300 (traceable). Unhappy customers: Too many. Loss of goodwill and reputation: No doubt, plenty.

The VP of operations learned of all this and called a meeting. "What the hell is going on here? Who's in charge of the problem?" "He is," said the sales manager pointing to the head of product engineering." "He is," said the head of product engineering pointing to the head of traffic. "He is," said the head of traffic pointing to the head of package engineering. "He is," said the head of package engineering pointing to the head of product engineering. "It's not a packaging problem. If we try to solve an engineering problem with a different package, it will cost us $9 over and above our budgeted packaging costs. If this is what you want, O.K."

The VP of operations ordered a unit brought into the meeting. He took off the cover, fiddled with the PC board, called for a screwdriver, and unscrewed the one lonely mounting screw. "Here's your damn problem," he said with exasperation. "This screw goes in three-eighths of an inch. It's supposed to screw in three-quarters of an inch. Somewhere, somehow, some nitwit changed the screw dimensions. The one we're using simply doesn't have enough bite." He glared at the group. "Now will someone be kind enough to tell me why the hell this small bit of information took four and a half months to find?"

"It certainly shouldn't have taken four and a half months," the group chorused in return, glaring at each other and warming up their pointing fingers for the next round.

Conclusion: It certainly shouldn't have taken four and a half months. There were two screw-ups: a screw screw-up and an organizational screw-up that permitted the screw screw-up to be screwed up so long.

Shortly afterward, I had lunch with the CEO of a very successful and well-managed computer company. "Incredible," he chuckled when I told him this story. "If it took those guys over four months to spot and correct a simple problem like that, I shudder to think what else they're missing. Their organization must resemble a cattle stampede." "Right you are, Trail Boss," I smirked maliciously. The chuckling came to an abrupt halt.

The fact is that, by comparative standards, his company is well run, efficient, and by and large tightly organized. It has an average growth rate of 36 percent for the previous four years. However, what this story illustrates is that in every organization, even the good ones, one whale of a lot of problems slide by, generally because of the elements of slow decision making we noted; in this case, caused by confusion about responsibility and by decision drift.

All this brings us to our next subject—reorganizing the decision-making process to reduce, if not prevent, this type of tempo-slowing situation. As noted before, what good is a "good" decision if by the time it's made the problem it was supposed to solve has become a catastrophe, perhaps requiring an entirely different decision, or if the opportunity it was supposed to take advantage of is long gone? Chapter 6 dealt with some typical case analyses and showed the effects of some of the 11 elements of organizational behavior that contribute to slow organizational tempo. The question now is whether we can devise a structure for decision making that will eliminate these elements (or their effects)?

THE IDEAL STRUCTURE FOR DECISION MAKING

If we were to delineate the ideal decision-making structure, we'd probably come up with something like this. It should:

- Create an environment in which decisions would flow as needed, and be timely in response to the problems or opportunities they address.
- Involve all levels of management, especially lower and

lower-middle, in the *creative* aspects of the decision-making process.

- Provide for the effective coordination between the various decision-making levels.
- Create an environment in which decisions would flow as needed, and be timely in response to the problems or opportunities—an environment in which there is a continuous forward thrust.
- Provide a simple, efficient communications system for keeping senior levels of management informed.
- Provide an environment for translating senior management's policies into action with a minimal loss of enthusiasm or intent.
- Provide a basis for assessing individual executive performance.
- Lend itself to a simple and effective administration.

If we bear these objectives in mind, then the following steps are called for.

1. Decision-making responsibility must be made specific, clear-cut, and not subject to evasion, confusion, or executive timidity.
2. Decisions must be given time limits to prevent decision drift.
3. Decision-making responsibility must be brought as close as is practicable to the levels where problems and opportunities exist.
4. The authority of the executive charged with making a decision must be as absolute as his responsibility, to permit him to get whatever assistance he feels he needs, *when* he feels he needs it.
5. The whole process must be held together with a simple communications system.
6. And finally, the whole process must lend itself to simple, constructive enforcement.

INTRODUCING MANAGEMENT BY DECISIONS

Put it all together and you get the basis for "Management by Decisions" (or MBD), the details of which we'll get into shortly. MBD was derived very simply by breaking the causes of slow organizational tempo (read "slow decision making") into the 11 elements already noted and then step by step devising a decision-making framework that structures these elements or their *effects* out. MBD is essentially a structural approach designed to give the process a high degree of operating permanence yet supple enough to adapt to changing organizational pressures and needs.

The base of MBD rests on three important facts. First is the recognition that no organization moves, solves problems, seizes opportunities, marshals and uses assets profitably, does anything (except maybe vegetate) without making decisions. Therefore, any effective process must establish the primacy of decision making as a corporate activity. If you think this primacy commonly exists now, consider this: You pump a matter in need of a decision into the present decision-making mill, and how this mill operates depends on the work habits and patterns of the executive team, the moods of its members, the aggressiveness and character of the organization, the number and types of problems and opportunities the process is currently wrestling with, and so on. In other words, the decision is now keyed to the *organization*. MBD recognizes the need to change this and key the organization's moods and so forth to its decision-making needs. Subtle as it may sound, there's a world of difference between the two approaches!

The second fact is this: Most executives can decide more incisively and faster if the proper environment is created and if higher levels of expectations are established and the means are created to meet these levels. In brief, I've found that most executives tend to operate at a pace considerably below their potential. MBD is designed to reverse this and provide the structure for most executives to function closer to full potential.

Third, as we unfold the details of MBD, you might begin to conclude that an executive in a system that continually puts pressure on its people to make faster and firmer decisions and judgments will feel so harassed and dehumanized ("Man is not a machine," you might feel the urge to say) that he and the system will eventually break down under the strain.

In truth, I've found that more ulcers are caused by the frustrations of slow decision making than by the requirements of fast decision making. The fact is that the longer the time lag between idea inception and its decision and implementation, the greater the loss of initial enthusiasm. And this loss of enthusiasm has become an insidious problem in most companies today. By bringing idea inception and decision closer together, we can hold on to this initial enthusiasm, and enthusiastic people are not generally unhappy, harassed people. A stepped-up tempo in seeing things happen, a greater opportunity for individual expression, a greater feeling of personal involvement, perhaps a greater understanding of corporate purpose as events unfold faster and closer together—these are the elements that promote good morale, good motivation, satisfaction, and self-fulfillment.

And as for dehumanization, we've all seen many executives in many organizations who are pretty dehumanized figures now. Often buffeted by executive competition, often victims of corporate factionalism, often insecure in their jobs, uncertain how to get recognition without stepping on someone else's toes and perhaps creating an enemy, not made to feel that they are an important part of a thriving organization, often shunted aside by the whims of others—this is the stuff that dehumanization is made of.

In most organizations, some executives of course rise above this. In an organization of 200 executives, perhaps 10 or 20 have the smarts, personality, and drive to crack the system. But what about the other 180 or 190? This "natural selection process" often rewards and lays greater stress on aggressiveness than on creativity. While aggressiveness *is* a virtue, and a pretty important one, the creative talents of others who are not so aggressive are often lost to the organization, and this represents a waste of organizational talent that few organizations can really afford.

MBD strives to provide the means by which many of these creative executives can make a far more effective contribution to the organization. As noted before, in the final analysis an organization is its people, and the big difference between one organization and another is how these people's efforts are marshaled and channeled. Despite its emphasis on structure, MBD is people oriented because it is designed to overcome specific human *weaknesses* and to give fuller play to latent human *strengths*.

Realistically, MBD is *not* for every manager. Experience has shown that some are overwhelmed by its requirements and simply not able to carry their share of the load. But in most cases, these will be people who are misplaced, a fact often obscured by the present system which permits, if not encourages, people to avoid decision-making responsibility.

THE MECHANICS OF MBD

Step 1: To ensure that decision-making responsibility will be specific, clear-cut, and not subject to confusion, executive timidity, or evasion.

This sounds, perhaps, like an organizational nirvana, but implementing it is not as difficult as it sounds. We simply assign decision-making responsibility to individuals on the basis of the *specific* decision areas for which they are responsible. This is the cornerstone of the program. The basic structure of the program is built on this.

Present job descriptions are traditionally couched in terms of *general* areas of responsibilities. The rationale behind this is of course that someone will be responsible for each area of a business and one need only consult the organization chart to find out who is responsible for what. Starting with the CEO, who is in charge of everything, large segments of responsibilities are delegated progressively downward for supervision and implementation, and reports on results then flow back up.

In theory, this sounds fine. In practice, though, it doesn't always work the way we would like to think it works. If it did, we wouldn't have to contend with the elements that slow organizational tempo. But the fact is job descriptions that outline general areas of responsibility create confusion over who is specifically responsible for what because of misinterpretation and overlap. This leads to incidences where decision-making responsibilities are split. And certainly, this opens the door to possible decision delay or evasion. So within certain limits, discard those job descriptions that deal with general areas of responsibility and adopt instead descriptions that define specific decision areas.

Before illustrating this new job description, let's define some new terms. Because under MBD a decision maker not only has responsibility for making the decision but also has unusual authority to put its elements together (I'll describe this process later), we call this fellow the "Decision Coordinating Authority" (or DCA). To make this responsibility unequivocal, the *only* person in the organization empowered to make the *initial* decision about a specific subject matter is the executive who has been assigned to that subject matter as its DCA. A superior can direct a problem to a DCA for decision, but he cannot at this time direct the outcome of that decision, only that one be made. If a DCA does not make the decisions for which he is responsible, or makes bad ones, his dereliction now becomes highly visible and that responsibility can be reassigned to someone else.

There's a very important underlying point here, and the above should be read with it in mind. We often confuse *au-*

thority with *responsibility*. We figure if someone has authority over a certain area, he has the responsibility for it and vice versa. We say, for example, "Ralph has the authority to buy paper clips." In MBD we create this critical distinction: The fact that Ralph has the authority to make a decision to buy paper clips doesn't necessarily mean he'll make the decision to buy them when they're needed. MBD, therefore, says, "Ralph has the *responsibility* to make the decision about buying paper clips when they're needed." One is permissive (he *can* make the decision); the other is obligatory (he *must* make the decision)—a subtle but very important point and the heart of MBD.

Now let's take a look at Exhibit 4—a partial job description under MBD of a plant manager of a small plant.

EXHIBIT 4. Partial job description under MBD for the manager of a small plant.

General: To manage and administer the physical plant, its production activities, and budgets for personnel and plant.

Specific: Decision areas are listed below.

Decision Area	DCA
Prepare quarterly plant budget	Plant manager
Salary adjustments (over and above quarterly budget)	
Up to 5%	Plant manager
Over 5%	Plant manager
Alterations to manufacturing equipment (single project) costing:	
Up to $1,000	Head, industrial engineering
$1,000 to $2,500	Production mgr.
Over $2,500	Plant manager

Decision Area	DCA
Purchase new manufacturing equipment costing:	
Up to $10,000	Plant manager
$10,000 to $30,000	Plant manager
Over $30,000	VP Mfg.
Approval, changes in basic raw materials	Plant manager
Approval, new sources of basic raw materials	Materials mgr.
Quarterly production schedule	Plant mgr.
Monthly production schedule	Production mgr.
Overtime authorization: (hrs/week/section)	
Up to 20	Section foremen
21 to 100	Production mgr.
Over 100	Plant mgr.

In Section 5 of the tempo questionnaire, we used the hypothetical case of a purchasing agent to whom an equipment salesman brought a new piece of equipment for consideration. We'll apply that situation to Step 1. In fact, for coherence, we'll use the same situation throughout this chapter, wherever possible.

Let's assume that the equipment costs $25,000. The purchasing agent checks his list of DCAs and finds that the plant manager is the appropriate one under the decision category: "Purchase new manufacturing equipment costing $10,000–30,000" (see Exhibit 4). He sends the new equipment data to the plant manager for the buy or not-to-buy decision. There's absolutely no question who is to coordinate the elements of the decision input and then make the decision. Simple, huh?

Step 2: To coordinate the various levels of responsibility.

In Step 1 we established that the DCA has the sole responsibility to make the *initial* decision. At the same time, it obviously makes little sense to give certain profit and functional responsibilities to senior or middle-management executives and then eliminate totally their control over a subordinate's decisions that would affect these responsibilities.

Yet, we seemingly did this in Step 1 by insisting that the plant manager be the only one empowered to make the *initial* (the key word) decision about this new piece of equipment.

Here in Step 2, we give this overall control back to his superior. In doing so, we do not take away the plant manager's responsibility (note again, not authority, but *responsibility*) to make that initial decision. We simply add the superior's. He comes on the scene in his role as an "Approval Authority," or AA for short. The superior who feels that he wants or needs final authority over certain decision areas becomes the approval authority. This gives him the authority to review, change, accept, or reject the DCA's decision, *after* the latter has discharged his responsibility by making it. Implementation of the DCA's decision, of course, must wait on this final approval.

Exhibit 5 illustrates how the role of the AA is introduced into the job description. Note that if the equipment costs, say, $4,000, the plant manager requires no approval for his decision. He is on his own. At $25,000, however, his DCA decision would go to the VP of manufacturing for approval, rejection, or amendment.

The rationale for this two-tier system lies in the following points.

1. Under our present system, common practice is for a subordinate to bring his superior a problem, perhaps a loose col-

EXHIBIT 5. Partial job description under MBD for the manager of a small plant with AA and second AA responsibilities added.

General: To manage and administer the physical plant, its production activities, and budgets for personnel and plant.

Specific: Decision areas are listed below.

Decision Area	DCA	AA	Second AA
Prepare quarterly plant budget	Plant manager	VP Mfg.	President
Salary adjustments (over and above quarterly budget)			
Up to 5%	Plant manager	None	
Over 5%	Plant manager	VP Mfg.	
Alterations to manufacturing equipment (single project) costing:			
Up to $1,000	Head, industrial engineering	Production mgr.	
$1,000 to $2,500	Production mgr.	Plant manager	
Over $2,500	Plant manager	VP Mfg.	
Purchase new manufacturing equipment costing:			
Up to $10,000	Plant manager	None	
$10,000 to $30,000	Plant manager	VP Mfg.	
Over $30,000	VP Mfg.	President	
Approval, changes in basic raw materials	Plant manager	VP Mfg.	Product mgr.
Approval, new sources of basic raw materials	Materials mgr.	Plant manager	
Quarterly production schedule	Plant mgr.	VP Mfg.	Product mgr.

EXHIBIT 5. Continued

General: To manage and administer the physical plant, its production
activities, and budgets for personnel and plant.
Specific: Decision areas are listed below.

Decision Area	DCA	AA	Second AA
Monthly production schedule	Production mgr.	Plant manager	Product mgr.
Overtime authorization: (hrs/week/section)			
Up to 20	Section foremen	Production mgr.	
21 to 100	Production mgr.	Plant manager	
Over 100	Plant mgr.	VP Mfg.	

---

lection of facts associated with it, and maybe a tentative recommendation, all of which becomes cohesive only if and when
the superior makes a decision. Under MBD this integration is
done at the subordinate level (by DCA decision, which must
be made *first*), and then the decision is dealt with as a whole
by the AA. Experience has clearly shown that an executive can
deal with such "packaged" decisions more effectively and with
greater perspective than if he has to start from scratch and become involved in the details of their construction, especially if
he is somewhat remote from the area under consideration. And
another reality of corporate life is that countless decisions either
die aborning or are neglected because executives remote from
the problem areas simply don't have the time, patience, or incentive to put all the decision's components together.

2. In theory, under our present system, the *final* decision
maker takes total responsibility for a decision (unless it turns
out to be a bad one, in which case he may try to parcel out
responsibility to whoever doesn't duck fast enough or hasn't
sufficiently covered himself.) Under MBD, if the AA approves

the DCA's decision, *both* share the responsibility (and/or credit) *equally* for its results—good, bad, or indifferent. But if the AA rejects or amends it, then he *alone* is responsible for its results. Thus, we have two people from two different levels who are *accountable* and must think creatively about the decision. And it's done with no confusion over who is responsible for what.

3. A high percentage of decisions made under our present system reflect what the decision maker thinks his boss might want or will accept. This creates a built-in psychological barrier to creative expression and idea initiative. Under MBD, because the decision and its construction are matters of record and can be used later as a basis for evaluating individual performance (as I'll explain more fully in a moment), a DCA tends to exercise his *own* judgment rather than simply mirror what he thinks will be his superior's thinking. This encourages initiative and creativity.

The reason for this is obvious. If the DCA makes a decision to do something and his AA rejects it, and time indicates that he was right and the AA was wrong, this fact will show up in the periodic evaluation of his decision packets. (A "decision packet" is the file kept by a DCA on all the components of a decision he makes including his decision and the AA's final decision. This will come into sharper focus when we discuss the role of memo writing in MBD a little later.) Under the present system, about the only way a subordinate can point out that he was right and his boss was wrong (where the boss makes the decision and the subordinate only contributes to it) is either to fight with his boss, which could be both devisive and impolitic, or to shoot a disloyal "I told him so" to someone else when his boss isn't looking. MBD eliminates the need for such tactics because now the subordinate, as DCA, has not only the opportunity but the *responsibility* to give the matter his best shot, uninfluenced by his boss, who doesn't even get to see it until the DCA has made the initial decision.

4. Under MBD and consistent with establishing the primacy

of getting decisions made, the DCA still maintains control over the decision's time frame. (I'll explain this shortly also.) The AA can vary only the content of the DCA's decision, *not* the time frame in which the DCA (or other initiator) says the decision must be made.

5. One of the factors that now leads to confusion about who's responsible for decisions is the tendency of many superiors to offhandedly make decisions ordinarily made by subordinates. A plant manager strolls through the plant. A foreman suggests they switch a machine around 90° to make more room for the operator. The plant manager offhandedly says, "Sure, go ahead." The department supervisor walks by later, sees the machine turned around, and asks, "How come?" "Plant manager told me to," is the reply. The supervisor shrugs, or cusses. Has he suddenly lost his authority to decide how his machines are placed? Should *he* make the decision the next time he wants to move a piece of equipment or pass it off to the plant manager? Confusion results—especially if his authority is repeatedly undermined by a plant manager who can't resist making a decision even if the authority properly belongs to a subordinate. Under MBD, once the mode of operation becomes a pattern, the tendency is for superiors to defer to subordinates (those with appropriate DCA responsibilities), even when the matter lends itself to being decided in an offhand way.

Or often someone will pull an end run around the decision maker and take the matter to the decision maker's boss for decision because he feels he'll get a more sympathetic hearing or he'll score a few Brownie points with the boss. Whatever the reason, this type of organizational bollix tends to diminish and is encouraged to disappear as DCA responsibilities become fixed.

6. A situation that often contributes to confusion and conflict, and thus decision delay, occurs when different departments or people of equal rank are involved in a decision, each with an interest in its results. For example, earlier I cited the

case of a new product package decision where there was a legitimate difference of opinion between the marketing manager and the production manager over the criteria of a good package. One wanted a package that would help sell his product; the other a package that was inexpensive to assemble and ship. In such cases, hemming and hawing and fussing and diddling while trying to resolve differences might prevent a decision from ever being made. Even a third-person arbiter could find himself caught in a cross fire of conflict, and the decision could drag out.

The DCA–AA relationship would act to smooth out such a problem by designating either the marketing manager or the production manager as the DCA and the other as the AA. Which would be which would depend on the marketing strategy of the company. And even here, if there is a third-person reviewer (an executive senior to the other two, possibly a second AA), he could find the way to a final decision smoother because he would now be dealing with firm viewpoints, not time-consuming arguments and rebuttals by the participants.

7. It will be noted in Exhibit 5 that we've introduced a second approval authority in certain areas. For example, the plant manager has the responsibility for preparing a quarterly plant budget. The VP of manufacturing has the responsibility for approving, rejecting, or changing it. The president, assuming he has reserved for himself the role of company coordinator for budgets, is listed as the second approval authority to give him this ultimate responsibility.

Or suppose the plant manager wants for economic reasons to change a product raw material, say, from steel to plastic. He makes the initial decision to do so. The VP of manufacturing reviews the decision as the AA, probably from the same product cost-savings perspective as the plant manager. However, because the decision might have an effect on the marketability of the product, the product manager is called in as the second approval authority, to weigh cost savings against any change in potential marketability, and has ultimate approval authority.

Ditto with, for example, quarterly production scheduling. The plant manager prepared a schedule. The VP of manufacturing, as AA, reviews and approves it. The product manager (or marketing manager or sales manager) gets to see it as the final (second) approval authority based on the assumption that he will be in the best position to relate it to his sales forecasts.

8. Finally, it should be restated that many DCA decisions require no AA approval.

Step 3: To set up a procedure to make decisions maximally responsive to the time needs of the problem or opportunities they address and to prevent decision drift.

Now that we've set up a relatively evasion-proof process for determining who's responsible for specific decisions and coordinated it between at least two levels of management, the next step is to prevent decisions coming out of that process from drifting. The most obvious and direct way is simply to set a date at the outset by which time the decision *must* be made. The setting of this date is the responsibility of either the person who brings the matter up for decision or the DCA.

Back to our $25,000 piece of new equipment. When the purchasing agent sends the DCA the data on the equipment, the DCA, *upon receipt,* sets a deadline for making the decision. This date is also binding on those people from whom he may request data and recommendations. It's also binding on the approval authority. At the outset, everyone involved knows not only who will make the initial decision and who will review it but also by *when* the decision will be made.

Let's go a step further and introduce a complication. Assume the equipment salesman tells the purchasing agent there is only one piece of equipment available and the next one won't be built for six months. "However," the salesman adds, "I can hold it for three weeks before offering it to a competitor." On the basis of this knowledge, the purchasing agent, as the decision initiator, sets the decision date at three weeks hence, and everyone, including the DCA, is now bound by that date. Again, this doesn't affect the content of the decision. For example, the DCA may think he needs more than three weeks to arrive at an intelligent decision to buy and as a result is willing to forgo the possible advantage of being first with the new equipment. So his decision is not to buy. If it's approved by the AA, then that's the decision, period.

Whether the decision is good, bad, or indifferent, the purpose of due dates is to ensure that a decision will be made—and that it will be made within a preset, fixed time frame. Of course, because the decision is now a matter of written record (and I'll explain the mechanics of this shortly), the DCA might not be so quick to come up with that kind of nowhere decision unless he had a pretty good reason; nor would the AA want to share the responsibility for such a decision, especially if someday the president might come along and ask pointedly, "How come our competitor has this piece of equipment when it was offered to us first?"

Step 4: To eliminate the remote decision maker and give real teeth to effective delegation.

We've already given effective delegation one set of choppers by establishing the role of DCAs. We give it a second set by selecting these DCAs from levels normally a rung or two below where certain decisions are presently made. This is usually closer to where the problems or opportunities are and where the impacts and nuances are perhaps best understood. The people who make those decisions under the present system generally become the approval authorities.

This is *real* delegation, where the results (in this case, DCA decisions) are evaluated and the methods and techniques used to arrive at those results are not evaluated during the process of developing the decision. Naturally, the AA might question the basis for the DCA's decision while reviewing a decision, but not while the DCA is developing it. The organization that evaluates results instead of techniques and methods not only tends to move faster but encourages more innovation, the development of problem-solving skills, and more active participation at all levels of management in identifying problem areas, finding problem solutions, and developing opportunities.

Step 5: To give the DCA authority to establish a time schedule for the decision-making process.

As noted, under MBD the date established at the outset by which a decision must be made is binding on all parties involved in contributing to the components of the decision—the DCA, the AA, data suppliers, and those whose recommendations are sought. As the decision *coordinating* authority, the DCA is charged with the responsibility for coordinating these inputs. He therefore has the authority, *given him by the decision due date*, to ask for data, recommendations, and ultimately a review by an AA in such time frames as to permit him to meet this decision due date. How this operates and is enforced will be made clearer shortly.

Step 6: To provide for a simple and effective administration of the MBD program.

Administration of the program falls into two categories: "compliance management" and "general administrative management."

Let's take compliance first. It's all very nice to lay out a program and detail responsibilities and procedures, but it doesn't mean anything unless that program has a full set of teeth. MBD will slip and backslide, as will any program that doesn't have an effective framework for achieving compliance.

In MBD, this framework is provided through the role of the "Decision Program Manager" (DPM). His job is to oversee the machinery for making decisions and keep it greased. Built into the essence of the program itself is the unique tool around which this compliance process functions: the use of decision due dates.

To see how this works, let's go back to our case example: The company's purchasing agent, after being solicited by the new equipment company's salesman, sends a "Decision Initiation Memo" (see Exhibit 6, later in chapter) to the plant manager, who is DCA for "purchase new manufacturing equipment costing $10,000–30,000." He indicates in the memo that a copy is going to the DPM and, for the reason he notes, he (the purchasing agent) rather than the DCA is setting the decision due date. That date now governs when the decision *must* be made. The DPM files the memo in a tickler file, and when the due date rolls around, if he doesn't have another memo indicating that the decision has in fact been made, he then knows that the due date was missed, and it's his job to find out who held it up and why.

The DPM should be high enough in rank and have enough clout so that when he asks questions about the missed deadline, the culprits will pay attention. Because MBD is devoted to the primacy of decision making as a corporate activity, the DPM should have a clear backup pipeline to senior managers (unless he is one himself) both for reporting purposes and so that any remedial action required can be taken as quickly and smoothly as the situation may call for. In a very real sense, he should be able to speak with top management's voice when it comes to ensuring the success of the program.

For example, suppose the plant manager has a pattern of missing due dates and it becomes pretty obvious to the DPM that the plant manager simply can't adapt to the decision-making requirements of MBD. Perhaps he is so disorganized that he just can't pull it all together in time, or perhaps he's carrying too many responsibilities or hasn't delegated sufficiently, or perhaps he's just too gun-shy to make hard and fast decisions. Whatever, it becomes the responsibility of the DPM to identify the cause and recommend an appropriate course of action, including replacement of the DCA.

Or he may find that the approval authority (in our example, the VP of manufacturing) tends to sit on decision approvals and that this accounts for the DCA's inability to file a final decision by its due date, or that people who were requested to provide data or recommendations didn't get back to the DCA in time, or that perhaps the DCA waited too long to ask for the information. The point is the reason for the missed date is traceable and, once traced, is correctable when the DPM does his job. (In practice, the DPM does not normally charge up on a white horse, saber flashing in the sun, every time a due date is missed. A goof-up here and there is to be expected, and if an executive doesn't make a habit of throwing sand into the decision-making gears, the occasional goof-up can be let go without stomping all over the offender's head—unless of course the decision goofed up was of sufficient importance that it shouldn't have been goofed up.)

Under our present system, where job descriptions outline general areas of responsibilities, if an executive boots it in a few areas, his superiors are apt to snarl and growl and bounce him out. MBD permits more selectivity in that the DPM may recommend reassignment of some of an executive's DCA or AA responsibilities. For example, perhaps the plant manager is a crackerjack production administrator, strong on manufacturing systems, cost controls, labor supervision, and the like. But maybe when it comes to making decisions relating to large expenditures, he is simply too timid. The DPM can, under these circumstances, recommend (or the plant manager's boss can direct) that the infrequent decisions regarding large expenditures be assigned to someone else as DCA—the VP of manufacturing, perhaps—and leave those DCA assignments with the plant manager where he's the strongest and most useful to the organization.

The DPM has a number of *administrative functions.*

1. In the event of a time conflict—as might happen, for example, when someone other than the DCA initiates a request for a decision and sets a due date the DCA feels for good reason he can't meet—the DPM would undertake to resolve the conflict. The DPM would also step in if the DCA requests some data that the respondent feels he can't get together in time and the two can't work it out. (Experience shows that this type of unresolved conflict is surprisingly rare. If DPM intervention is frequently required, I've found that the source of the conflict tends to go deeper than a dispute over the timing of individual inputs.) If the decision initiator refiles a Decision Initiation Memo to change the original due date to a later one, the DPM, if he feels the change will compromise the original intent of the decision or its effectiveness, is responsible for examining the reasons given and hollering if he's unhappy with the explanation.

2. Companies that have a rapid growth rate sometimes develop responsibility vacuums as new decision areas arise. The DPM is charged with recommending appropriate new DCA or AA assignments to fill the vacuums. An executive may get promoted or fired, leaving some decision-making responsibilities hanging in limbo. The DPM might recommend not filling the job and parceling the responsibilities out to others instead.

3. We noted that the DPM is also charged with the responsibility of recommending DCA and AA assignments when DCAs or AAs can't handle their assignments under MBD. In another application, the DPM may recommend changes designed to keep the company flexible and light on its feet in responding to changing conditions without requiring a major disruptive reorganization. For example, if a division of a company is drifting from an R&D orientation to a marketing one because of the completion of product line development, the DPM, or someone else, might spot the need to shift certain decision-making responsibilities in response to this changing need. This can be done by simply reassigning certain DCA or

AA assignments from R&D executives to the appropriate marketing executives, again without necessitating a major reorganization. (One three-division organization wanted to decentralize. Excessive corporate authority, it felt, was impinging on the entrepreneurial abilities of the divisional general managers. Without going through the pangs of an involved reorganization, it simply slid some DCA and AA assignments gradually from the corporate to the division level, until it was satisfied that it had hit on the right combination. There was never any confusion during the transition period over who was responsible for what decisions at any one time.)

4. The DPM is essentially responsible for the decision tempo of the organization, especially at middle and lower levels. Therefore, one of his most important jobs is to check constantly to make sure that decision due dates are kept sufficiently tight. If he sees that a decision is due in one month and he thinks it can and should be made in one week, it's up to him to push for the earlier date. If he discerns a pattern of widening due dates developing, it's his job to find out why and to take steps to reverse the pattern. It's up to him to prevent decision due dates from becoming too comfortable. In this facet of administration, his job is uniquely more art than science.

5. And finally, the DPM is responsible for seeing that lists of DCA and AA assignments are kept current and properly disseminated, so everyone with decision responsibility knows exactly what he's responsible for and, just as important, so does everyone else.

One final note: The rank of the DPM and the number of DPMs in an organization can vary. A large organization, segmented into various operating divisions, each with a great deal of autonomy, may, for example, have a full-time DPM for each division. At the other end of the spectrum, the president of one company (320 employees) serves as his own DPM on a part-time basis. In any case, the DPM's job should never be regarded as a slot to be filled by someone's brother-in-law because no one knows what else to do with him. Being a DPM is not a low-level job unless the organization doesn't really care what happens to its tempo.

Step 7: To provide a communications system to keep top management and profit center, line, and staff heads informed.

One of the most time-consuming jobs of senior management (estimated at anywhere from 30 to 70 percent of an executive's time) is keeping informed on important events and trends taking place within the company. Most who try to do this by bottom-line reports often find they're dealing with results long after the fact. Others spend an inordinate amount of time in meetings designed to find out what's happening. Sorting out the important from the unimportant is a big part of the problem.

Score another point for MBD. After pinpointing the areas about which they feel they must be kept informed, appropriate executives can direct that they be sent copies of all decisions for which certain other executives are the approval authorities. These copies are for information only and are normally sent right *after* the decisions are made. For example, the president might direct that copies of those decisions for which his vice presidents or division heads are AAs be sent to him on the theory that if a decision requires a VP's approval, then it's important enough for the president to at least be aware of it. Similarly, the VP of marketing can direct that all copies of decisions for which his product managers and other key marketing executives are AAs be sent to him for information.

Or a senior executive may want to keep tabs on a department, perhaps a problem one, and not let things there get too far out in front of him. He can simply direct that he get copies of decisions from whatever levels he thinks necessary. Or he may feel that the problems cannot be corrected without his personal intervention. If so, he can assign himself for as long as he wants as a second AA with final decision authority. (In this case, if he approves the AA's decision, who in turn has approved the DCA's decision, then all three share responsibility and/or credit for its results. If he changes or rejects the first AA's decision, then it's his ball game and his responsibility. If the first AA has rejected the DCA's decision, and the second AA agrees with the DCA's decision, then both the DCA and the second AA share responsibility for the results.)

Some executives may feel that they need to know what's going on in some department in order to coordinate their efforts with it. For example, the treasurer might want to keep informed of all projected large expenditures. By going through the lists of AA responsibilities, he can pick out the ones that involve large expenditures and have copies of just those decisions sent to him for information.

If the merit of any decision is questioned by a senior executive and he wants to check the basis for the decision, he need only send for the decision packet. This will give him the opportunity to assess the judgment used by the decision makers (both DCA and AA) and to examine the data used to arrive at the decision.

Step 8: To smooth the pathway for translating top management's policies into action quickly with minimal loss of enthusiasm or intent.

It's pretty tough to quarrel with the fact that, after drifting down the organizational pyramid to the various implementation levels, top-level project or policy decisions do not always come out the other end as top management originally intended. (Of course, in many cases decisions are improved, since one step may reveal a better way for the steps that follow, or new vistas may open that top management didn't perceive in its original thinking.)

A case in point that happened while this book was being written: The president of a truck parts jobber (the largest on the East Coast), with a relatively small executive staff, decided that his company should enter the marine market. He found that many truck part lines, especially engine and electrical lines, overlapped. By the end of six months, he figured, they should have a pretty good bite on the local market. He called a meeting of his sales manager, purchasing agent, and executive VP and outlined his plan. "We've got some basic overlapping lines already. We'll round those out with some strictly marine lines, and we'll be off and running." "We'll cream the market," his troops gurgled. "Fine," said the president. "You three put it all together."

A month and a half later, he called another meeting to see what progress had been made. Zilch. The sales manager, busy with his regular duties, was waiting for the purchasing agent to contract for some new marine lines, and the purchasing agent, busy with his regular duties, was waiting for the sales manager to tell him just what new lines to try to contract for. The executive VP, busy with his regular duties, and supervising the building of a new warehouse besides, somehow never found the time to straighten the mess out. Raising a gallon and a half of hell, the president told them they'd better get hot on the project.

Three weeks later, there had been a lot of motion, but the project itself had moved only inches. As time drifted by, the project that they went into with such enthusiasm became an irritating burden to the three implementors. They found it harder and harder to leave the starting line. They'd lost the directional thrust of the project as well as their initial enthusiasm.

Exasperated, the president finally reorganized the effort in a very simple, direct way: He gave the sales manager one week to find out what the market needed in new lines compatible with their present lines—"or else." At the end of that week, he gave the purchasing agent four weeks to contract for distribution of the new lines—"or else." At the same time, he gave the sales manager three weeks to hire a couple of marine-market-oriented salesmen—"or else." He gave the executive VP two weeks to find another job—no "or else." Within seven weeks, they bulled their way into the marine market—not with as extensive a penetration as the president had originally hoped for, but at least they were off and running.

This type of situation where a project takes so long to get moving is another one of those things that "shouldn't happen in a well-run business." The fact is, of course, that this company didn't get to be the biggest in its field by sitting and watching the bluebirds go by. It *is* well run, with a strong aggressive owner-president. But these things *do* happen, and when the president first asked what was happening, he was beguiled by "We're working on it. As soon as I get some information from so-and-so, I'll take the next step." The president was at the same time setting up an export deal and, given this type of reassurance, didn't think he needed to follow up in any greater depth and take time away from his own project. Only when it became painfully apparent that nothing substantive was getting done did he demand a definitive progress report and start his whip-cracking campaign. This is not untypical of the type of slippage I've referred to throughout this book—the "shouldn't happen but somehow does."

MBD essentially provides as normal organization what the president had to do as a desk-banging reorganization of the project. As soon as the need was spotted, the sales manager would have been appointed DCA for a new decision area, "evaluation of marine market needs." He then would have had the responsibility for making this evaluation, and it would have been done within a time frame established at the outset of the project, with no confusion and no opportunity for him to slip this responsibility to the purchasing agent. This phase of the project would have been given a deadline within the time frame of the president's original decision—namely, "We will enter the marine market within six months."

MBD, in short, provides the machinery into which projects can be plugged without confusion and within time limits so that project initiation, development, and implementation are directly and tightly connected. If time limits (decision due dates) are sufficiently tight, not only can initial enthusiasm be held on to (as the idea unfolds into something concrete), but project momentum, after a fast break from the starting line, tends to mount steadily.

Step 9: To create a fertile environment for developing objectives.

Throughout, we have stressed the importance of individual responsibility, authority, and recognition designed not only to get things done but to encourage *creative* participation in the decision-making process, especially by lower levels of management. At the same time, it's hardly a secret that many, if not most, good ideas come out of one-on-one or group discussions in which word and idea triggers are pulled, pyramiding up to someone's "Flash! I've got a great idea!" This idea then becomes an objective if and when someone finally says, "O.K., let's do it!"

MBD creates a fertile environment in which objectives can develop from these group efforts. One of the weaknesses of *management by objectives* is its emphasis on the one-on-one (boss–subordinate) development of objectives. Unhappily, this often isolates the subordinate, who has too much riding (job, promotion, pay raises) on his own ability to come up with objectives to properly coordinate or even cooperate and trade off with others in the interest of achieving perhaps larger common objectives. There are some advantages, therefore, in developing objectives in a group. It permits everyone to know how he fits into an overall program, how one objective will tie into another, how the members of the group can support one another, and what is expected from each. It tends to produce mutually supportive objectives by consensus.

Yet, we've all been down this road often enough: A group meets, perhaps listens to some reports, and kicks around some ideas of which one or two sound good. Unless there's a pretty firm hand at the helm, at the end of the meeting everyone walks out with only some nebulous directions for follow-up. "We ought to look into it." (Who? When?) "That's a good idea. Let's think about it and kick it around some more next time." (Who, when, and often by the time "next time" rolls around, what?)

The fact is, of course, that good ideas turn into objectives only *if* they're put on a path that leads to decisions. One of the worst dampeners of creative thought in our corporate society is the "Aw, hell, what's the use?" syndrome. A salesman out in the field comes up with what he thinks is a great idea to generate a whole lot of new business. At the next sales meeting in Sheboygan, he mentions it to his sales manager who nods his head and smiles. "Sounds good," he says, rushing for the door. "Let me think about it." End of the line. The salesman hears no more. Sometime later he may ask the sales manager whatever happened to his idea and then get the feeling that the sales manager is rejecting it right there with the first reason he can think of simply because he hasn't given it any thought up to that point and doesn't want to admit it. This happens a few more times, and pretty soon the salesman stops thinking. Or if he gets another idea, despite his best efforts not to, he quickly shelves it, thinking "Boy, if only they'd listen to me."

This syndrome is endemic in many organizations. Ask several people individually what's wrong with the company or their department, and, if you can get them to open up, chances are everybody will have some pretty firm opinions they've been brooding about. "Why haven't you told anyone?" You guessed it. "Aw, hell, what's the use?"

There's no way to totally eliminate this attitude, such are the realities of human frailties. MBD, however, tends to reduce it, since group meetings are targeted for decisions rather than for open-ended trips to the land of nowhere. This is possible because job descriptions define specific decision responsibilities and decision due dates are required. When an idea is presented within this framework, one person, known to all, is responsible for making a decision and a due date is established at the point the idea is presented (or shortly thereafter).

We'll talk about how it works, but first, let's see how it doesn't work, so we can have a basis for comparison.

A group of executives meet in an interdepartmental staff meeting.

Purchasing agent: "I know this is out of my province, but I saw some sales figures the other day on our meter line, and it looks to me like our market is shifting from oil refineries to ultilities. The sales curve is down on one, edging up on the other. Shouldn't we shift with the trend and put more effort into selling utilities?"

Marketing manager: "Well, we're looking into that now. But bear this in mind: Oil refineries aren't as tight with their money as utilities and it costs less to sell them, and we can make a better markup. We are on top of it, however."

After the meeting, the marketing manager asks his sales manager, "What did you think of that idea?"

Sales manager: "I haven't really looked at the figures in that light, but what the hell does he know about our markets. Oil refineries have always been our primary market. We know it. We're geared for it, and we have a better than 60 percent share of it. We've got a lot of years of good contacts built up there. If we dilute our sales effort, we're apt to find ourselves aced out of both markets."

Marketing manager: "Well, think about it and let me know. He may have a point."

Sales manager: "Sure."

This example is based on fact. The sales manager did nothing, and aside from prodding him with one or two half-hearted reminders, the marketing manager also did nothing. Two years later, after a decline in the sales curve as the refinery market tightened up, the marketing manager got the boot. The new marketing manager spotted the trend as meaningful and applied more muscle to the utility market, dividing the sales effort into two divisions, refineries and utilities, and hiring a new sales manager for the latter. But the company now had to play catch-up, which was both costly and time consuming. This type of case is not especially rare.

Now let's project what would have happened under MBD. After the purchasing agent made his suggestion and it was initially judged as having possible merit, the chairman of the meeting would have noted, "Mr. Sales Manager, you're the DCA for 'evaluation, new markets.' Why don't you review the figures and get back to us at our next meeting in two weeks with a decision on what course of action you decide to take." The chairman makes a note of the idea and follow-up decision date, or if he wishes, he can make it more formal and write out a Decision Initiation Memo (see Exhibit 6) and send a copy to the decision program manager.

The sales manager, as DCA, is now under the gun to put effort and thought into evaluating the idea. His decision becomes a matter of record, and unless he's a complete dummy, he won't approach it in an offhand way. The VP of manufacturing, as the approval authority, would also participate in the decision.

The point of all this is, of course, that the purchasing agent (and every other executive) has now, by means of a very simple and obvious device, been encouraged to think creatively about *all* the company's problems and opportunities because he has a defined forum for his ideas. He knows in advance that his idea, if he pushes it, will not just drift off into the mist but will come back to him full circle where he can see some fruit of his effort in the form of a decision. Thus does

EXHIBIT 6. Example of Decision Initiation Memo.

DECISION DUE DATE:___6/10___

FILE NUMBER:___JJ–5/20-1___

DATE:_____5/20_____

FROM: Jack Jones, Purchasing

TO: Bill Brown, Plant Manager, Bloomington
          DCA for purchase of new manufacturing equipment costing
          $10,000–$30,000

CC: Sam Black, VP Manufacturing—AA
          Decision Program Manager

SUBJECT: Enclosed is catalog data sheet and other material on new
          punch press just coming on the market for $25,000, which
          manufacturer claims can increase our production rate 20% with
          no increase in operating costs. Sounds impressive. I have asked
          mfr's technical people to contact you. If you don't hear from
          them by 5/25, let me know. I've set the decision due date
          above on the basis of the salesman's claim that, while this one
          is available now, the next won't be for 6 months. He can hold
          this one for 3 weeks, after which he has to offer it to one of
          our competitors. I know this guy and credit his word. Al-
          though it's the first of a series, he assures me that it has been
          completely debugged. He can arrange for you to visit their
          plant to see it in operation.

Decision to be made: To buy or not to buy the above equipment.

DECISION: __✓__ requires   _____ does not require   approval.

                                  Signed _____
                                                Jack Jones

Notes: The DPM gets a copy for his tickler file, and the VP Manufacturing gets a copy simply to let him know that the DCA is working on a
decision involving this new piece of equipment. The decision due date
gives the DCA the authority to get whatever inputs he needs when he
needs them and is binding on him as well as on the AA.

MBD encourage this facet of creative participative management in a highly visible, highly satisfying sense.

Here's another case where MBD was used to generate new ideas and objectives: A company had had a suggestion box system for 12 years for the troops on the production line. As time went on, the number of suggestions dwindled, as more and more of those who were supposed to respond to the suggestions either lost interest, "couldn't find the time" to follow through, or just plain didn't think it was important enough and either ignored the need to reply or sloughed it off on some subordinate. The subordinates, having no authority to do anything about the suggestions even if they wanted to, found all kinds of reasons to reject them.

It came as no surprise to a new general manager when he analyzed one month's suggestion box contents to find that a large percentage of responses were anonymous, sometimes bitter suggestions as to what management could do with its suggestion boxes and other things. Many others were terse political statements or editorial comments on totally irrelevant matters.

The company instituted an MBD program. As part of it, the general manager assigned the decision program manager (a particularly tough-minded person) the job of reviewing the suggestions and assigning the ones that seemed to have some merit to the appropriate DCAs. At the same time, the DPM set the due dates as the decision initiator. When decisions came back to him, he saw to it that each was discussed with the person who made the original suggestion. If he felt that a decision was merely a slough-off, he would bounce it back to the DCA with the admonition that he reevaluate and resubmit it. If the DCA's decision was to respond positively to a suggestion, the DPM followed through to make sure it was properly implemented. The impact on morale along the production lines, if not dramatic, was at least significant, resulting in an increased number of highly innovative and useful suggestions.

One of these, by a lathe operator, opened up a whole new market for one of the company's product lines.

Step 10: To use MBD as a basis for assessing individual executive performance.

It follows that, if the primary activity of an organization is to make decisions and it's the role of individual executives to make those decisions, then essentially how they make decisions is an indication of how well they're doing their jobs. And here's where decision packets can play an important role.

For example, Wilbur is a product manager. In the past year, he's made many decisions. Further, he's been called on to make recommendations for decisions the final responsibility for which belonged to others. Much of this is included in his file of decision packets. They can tell us a whole lot about Wilbur. He might have made some decisions or recommendations that worked out fine—and others, not so fine. Some, for example, might have been rejected by an approval authority but in retrospect been proved right. Score six points for old Wilbur. Maybe senior management will conclude that the company ought to give his views more credence.

The point is, little of what Wilbur did as a contributor to the organization's health, good or bad, is lost. Evaluation of his decision packets can tell us how imaginative and incisive his decisions were, how often he met or beat his due dates, and thus how he contributed to the organization's tempo. They can tell us how aggressive and creative his decision follow-ups (implementations) were, something about his ability to analyze problems and opportunities, and something about his ability to grasp the big picture.

There is no set format for using decision packets in performance evaluations. One company has the executive to be evaluated indicate in one or two sentences how he thinks each of his decisions and recommendations did or didn't work out. His department head then makes his own notes, indicating, among other things, *his* appraisal of the results. These annotated packets then go to an evaluation board consisting of three senior executives (twice a year for promotions and pay increases). An interview with the person in question generally follows. If the department head rejects the conclusions of the board, they battle it out in conference.

One new president, taking over a company riven by politics and factionalism, a legacy of the old president, set up a procedure where, if a senior fires or approves the firing of a subordinate, the latter's decision packets are reviewed before final action is taken to help determine if the firing was justified, capricious, or in retaliation for betting on the wrong side. (In several cases, the subordinate was transferred to another department or division. In two cases, the people doing the firing got axed and the subordinates ended up being promoted into their jobs.)

Another organization has its department heads review their own people, with one senior executive reviewing their reviews. The combinations are endless and should be, like everything else, tailored to the organization, its objectives, and its personality.

Step 11. To tie the MBD program together with a simple communications system.

In its simplest terms, communications is a system of conveying information from one point to another. MBD does it by five types of memos:

1. Decision Initiation Memos (Exhibits 6 and 7).
2. Decision Recommendation and Data Memos (Exhibit 8).
3. Decision Recommendation and Data Reply Memos (Exhibit 9).
4. Decision Approval Request Memos (Exhibit 10).
5. Final Decision Memos (Exhibit 11).

The memo forms are preprinted with headings for the information to be filled in. The following examples (again using our case example) illustrate their use.

EXHIBIT 7. Example of Decision Initiation Memo format to be used if the purchasing agent does not issue a Decision Initiation Memo and the DCA does.

DECISION DUE DATE: 6/10

FILE NUMBER: BB–5/20-1

DATE: 5/20

FROM: Bill Brown, Plant Manager, Bloomington
          DCA for purchase of new manufacturing equipment
          costing $10,000–$30,000

TO: Decision Program Manager

CC: Sam Black, VP Manufacturing—AA
          Jack Jones, Purchasing

SUBJECT: Jack Jones sent me catalog and other data on new punch press.
          There's only one available now. Next one will be available
          in about 6 months. I have to make a decision in 3 weeks or,
          I've been told, equipment will be offered to a competitor.
          From what I can see, there's a good possibility we can in-
          crease our production rate by as much as 20% with little or
          no increase in cost.

Decision to be made: To buy or not to buy the above equipment.

DECISION: ___✓___ requires   _____ does not require   approval.

Signed _____
                                Bill Brown

Notes: This form, when used by the DCA as the decision initiator, simply plugs the decision into the formal MBD program. The decision due date gives him the authority to get inputs when he needs them and is also binding on the AA.

EXHIBIT 8. Example of Decision Recommendation and Data Memo.

DECISION DUE DATE:	6/10
I MUST HAVE YOUR REPLY BY	6/3
FILE NUMBER:	JJ–5/20-1
DATE:	5/25

FROM: Bill Brown, Plant Manager, Bloomington
            DCA for purchase of new manufacturing equipment
            costing $10,000–$30,000

TO: George Green, Industrial Engineering

REFERENCE: Attached copy of Decision Initiation Memo and punch press
           literature

I need from you:

> Your evaluation of cost to operate this press, utilities man-
> power, etc.
> How we would handle production flow; cost of additional
> materials handling equipment, if any.
> Where you would recommend we locate press if we buy.
> Your recommendation on whether to buy or not, and your
> reasons.

> Two of mfr's technical people will be in my office at 10 AM
> on 5/27. Please plan to join us. I understand press is oper-
> ating on their floor. We can arrange for one or both of us to
> see it in operation. I'll discuss this with you after we meet
> with these people.

Signed _____
                            Bill Brown

EXHIBIT 9. Example of Decision Recommendation and Data Reply Memo.

DECISION DUE DATE:	6/10
MY REPLY IS DUE:	6/3
FILE NUMBER:	JJ–5/20-1
DATE:	6/3

FROM: George Green, Industrial Engineering

TO: Bill Brown, Plant Manager, Bloomington—DCA

CC: Bob Blue, Production Supervisor

MY REPLY: Went over this with Bob Blue. He suggests, and I agree, press would go in aisle 3 where the two old welding machines are that we haven't used in years. Suggest scrapping those.

Although they claim a potential 20% production rate increase, based on what we saw at their plant, I can only see a 12% reduction. I think they underestimated our present rate. They're probably close to being right when it comes to running costs. Manpower will be the same and the added horsepower will only take about $20/week more current.

All we need for additional handling equipment is a slightly longer, 20 ft., conveyor so we can feed production from the press over the aisle into the assembly line. We've got this conveyor in the stockroom. No problem.

I'm still not happy with the control panel. It should be moved down at least 8 inches so our guys won't have to reach so far each shot. That can be tiring. I don't see why the mfr. can't do it. If they can't, or won't, we can—and should before we start operation.

I suggest we buy it. We're going to have to replace #4 press soon, as we discussed. This should make a good clean cost-savings replacement.

Signed _____
                    George Green

EXHIBIT 10. Example of Decision Approval Request Memo.

DECISION DUE DATE: __6/10__

FILE NUMBER: __JJ–5/20-1__

DATE: _____6/6_____

FROM: Bill Brown, Plant Manager, Bloomington
DCA for purchase of new manufacturing equipment costing $10,000–$30,000

TO: Sam Black, VP Manufacturing—Approval Authority

REFERENCE: Enclosed Decision Initiation Memo and other data

MY DECISION: Buy the press.

We plan to locate it in aisle 3, as George Green suggested. I accept his outline for handling production. Estimate use of press will reduce manpower overall in our punch press dept. by about 29 hours/week (see my basis for this attached) @ $12/hour = $17,700 per year. Additional utility costs about $1,000 per year because of higher power usage. Installation costs estimated at $2,700 including freight. (See schedule attached.) George and I have seen equipment operate on mfr's floor. Works as they said it would. We have no reason to believe it won't work as well here.

Signed _____
Bill Brown, DCA

YOUR DECISION IS: __✓__ approved _____ rejected _____ amended as below

I'm approving your decision but I question your installation costs. I'm adding another $1,000 to them in the budget to play safe. Also, check the noise factor. Heavier shock mounts may be needed to avoid exceeding our OSHA noise limits again. Let me know when it's due in.

Signed _____
Sam Black, Approval Authority

DATE RETURNED: ____6/10____

WHEN TO USE THE MBD PROGRAM

Most organizations make literally hundreds, if not thousands, of decisions daily. Many of these are repetitive and routine, such as updating production schedules and reordering standard parts. Most of the others, such as whether to buy red or green blotters or whether to work a crew overtime, are not of major importance.

Obviously, if every one of these went through the formalized program (the memo route, DPM involvement, and the like), the program would end up gurgling like a lead weight in a tub full of quicksand. This is neither practical, realistic, nor what the program really intends. What it does intend is that the bulk of an organization's decisions be made quickly and by the people assigned to make them.

Decisions that would go the formal route generally meet one or more of the following conditions:

1. The decision is of substantial importance to the company.

2. Time is an important factor in maximizing the effectiveness of the decision, and either the initiator or the DCA (if he's not the initiator) foresees a problem in getting the decision made promptly.

3. Many departments or individuals will be involved, and the DCA anticipates that a cooperation or coordination problem might arise that could slow down the decision making.

4. Either the initiator or the DCA feels that the decision is of such a type or magnitude that a written record is either desirable or necessary.

5. The DCA feels that he wants to make his judgment a matter of written record.

In short, whether to use the formalized memo and DPM involvement parts of the program for a particular decision is a matter of judgment by the initiator or the DCA. If a DCA chooses not to use it and to proceed informally, the responsibility for any failure to make the decision timely is still his.

EXHIBIT 11. Example of Final Decision Memo.

	DECISION DUE DATE: 6/10
	FILE NUMBER: JJ–5/20-1
	DATE: 6/10

FROM: Bill Brown, Plant Manager, Bloomington
                 DCA for purchase of new manufacturing equip-
                 ment costing $10,000–$30,000

TO: Jack Jones, Purchasing Agent, Decision Initia-
                 tor—for action
                 George Green, Industrial Engineering—for action
                 Sam Black, VP Manufacturing, Approval Author-
                 ity—for information only
                 DPM—for decision closeout
                 Bob Blue, Production Supervisor—for action

Jack Jones: Your Decision Initiation Memo #JJ–5/20-1 refers.
                   You are directed to purchase referenced equip-
                   ment. Your authority: the attached Decision Ap-
                   proval Request Memo. Please note: When
                   George Green and I met with equipment tech-
                   nical service people, they made all kinds of
                   promises of help in installation and training.
                   Please get this commitment spelled out in writing
                   as part of the purchase order and send George
                   and me a copy. Get exact date and time of deliv-
                   ery so we can schedule installation. We'll need
                   at least 2 days' notice.

George Green: You will handle installation, both equipment and
                   conveyor setup. Your budget: Not to exceed
                   $3,700. The mfr. will lower the control panel
                   as you requested. See Sam Black's note regard-
                   ing noise level. Please handle it and get me a db
                   reading when equipment is installed.

Tentative target dates: Equipment arrival—6/20
                          Installation—6/20–6/25
                          Completion of shakedown, including personnel
                          training—6/30
                          Operational—7/1

If you think you'll have any problems meeting these dates, let me know.
Reminder: Have someone from maintenance present during installation
so they can ask technical service people whatever they might need to
ask.

Bob Blue: This is press we discussed with you. I'll let you
                          know at least two days in advance when equip-
                          ment is due in. Please assign 4 people to be
                          trained in its operation. Make them good people.
                          We want to get the most out of this press we
                          can. I figure one man each shift and a backup
                          for each. If you disagree, let me know. The mfr.
                          has promised us at least 2 days' training. When
                          they come in for the installation, make your own
                          arrangements with them. If you have any prob-
                          lems, let me know.

                                        Signed _____
                                               Bill Brown, DCA

The point is, of course, that the program is available to the
DCA and his choice not to use it does not relieve him of his
decision-making responsibility.

  If the DPM notes that decisions that should follow the formalized route are beginning to slide around the program, it is
his job to tighten the ground rules. It should be stressed, however, that those decisions handled informally are still bound
by certain rules. The DCA still has the *sole* responsibility to
make the initial decision and, if required by his job description, to submit a firm decision to the AA for approval.

EVALUATING MBD

As Exhibits 12 and 13 show, MBD touches all the right bases and therefore ought to do pretty much what it is intended to do so far as corporate tempo is concerned. From this we might conclude, in a flight of unbridled enthusiasm, that MBD must be the closest thing to the perfect, infallible decision-making process system. And if you buy that, then we ought to get together to discuss some great opportunities we have in slightly salted gold mines and slightly damp swampland. The fact is, of course, that MBD can go wrong like any other management technique. It still takes people and commitment to make it work. The one advantage it does have over other management techniques is that its structure, if implemented properly, does touch those right bases.

EXHIBIT 12. How organizational tempo slowers are structured out by MBD.

Slowing element	Structured out by
1. Timidity	Reducing effect by assigning unequivocal responsibility for each decision area to a specific DCA so that decision responsibility cannot be evaded.
2. Incompetence	DCA assignments that quickly render incompetencies visible; permits reassignment of DCA or AA responsibilities.
3. Vague decision-making responsibility	DCA and AA assignments.
4. Decision drift	initiator's authority (or DCA's responsibility) to set decision date at inception with DPM for follow-up.
5. Remote decision maker	Moving DCA responsibilities closer to problem and opportunity levels.

Slowing element	Structured out by
6. Loss of decision-making momentum	Setting tight decision due dates at inception, with DPM follow-up; generally limiting decision-making authority to two executives (DCA and AA), with others along the chain acting as decision contributors, not potential stoppers.
7. Improper delegation	Assigning unequivocal decision-making responsibility to DCAs at levels closest to problems and opportunities.
8. Lack of authority commensurate with responsibility to get decision inputs in fixed time frame	Establishing DCA's authority to coordinate decision inputs by decision due date, with DPM follow-up.
9. Corporate politics and factionalism.	Blunting its *effect* by establishing DCA's authority to coordinate decision inputs from others; assigning unequivocal decision-making responsibility to DCAs; putting time limits on decision input; DPM follow-up.
10. Long lead times between decision and implementation	Providing time frames for implementation, with DPM follow-up
11. Organizational personality	All of above in establishing primacy of decision making (with appropriate compliance procedures) as a corporate activity.

Despite the fact that MBD's effectiveness cannot be measured in precise numbers (because we're dealing with gradations of before-and-after effectiveness and with varying degrees of program implementation), we can draw some broad conclusions based on results to date. In general, where it has worked (and it didn't in three cases, which we'll discuss shortly), the step-up in tempo has been obvious and in some

EXHIBIT 13. How MBD meets the objectives of a more effective decision-making process.

Objective	Met by
1. To ensure decisions will flow as needed	Unequivocal responsibility to one person (DCA) for each specific decision area, with DPM follow-up
2. To provide time frame to maximize effectiveness of decisions	DCA responsibility for setting time frame at inception; authority of initiator to set decision date; DPM follow-up.
3. To get lower management involved in creative decision making	DCA responsibilities to make initial decisions; lowering decision-making levels closer to problems and opportunities.
4. To coordinate between decision-making levels	Establishing the two-tier system (DCA–AA) of decision making, with provision for additional tier (second AA) as required.
5. To keep top management informed	AA submission to senior executives of decisions made at appropriate levels.
6. To create a more fertile environment for setting objectives	Providing action-oriented framework (DCAs, AAs, decision due dates, DPM follow-up) into which objectives can be plugged without confusion or unnecessary delay.
7. To permit top management's policy decisions to be translated into action with minimal loss of intent	See 6 above.
8. To assess individual executive performance	Analysis and evaluation of DCA and AA decision packets.
9. To provide for simple administration of the process	Establishment of decision program manager and appropriate compliance and administrative procedures.

cases, dramatic. Decisions that took weeks or months to make (if they ever got made at all) are often now made in days. And the decisions are generally more incisive than previously and more responsive to the problems and opportunities they address. Projects, by and large, are enunciated and implemented faster. In at least three cases, the resultant streamlining permitted a reduction in the total number of managers, since the remaining managers were able to enlarge the scope of their responsibilities with little or no additional time input. As the program has become a focal point for management effort, there has been a perceptible decrease in any previous preoccupation with company politics, resulting in better coordination and mutual support between departments and individuals.

In two cases, some significant and wrenching changes in management personnel were necessary. In both cases, the organizations had been mired in inertia, and it was a matter of either replacing the people who just couldn't leave ground zero or accepting a continued slide in the bottom lines to disaster. Both companies opted for the first alternative, and after a brief (and in one case, turbulent) readjustment period (about four months for one, seven to eight months for the other), the turnaround effects became apparent.

Even in two cases where the program was limited to a simple rewriting of job descriptions by specific decision areas (with DCA and AA responsibilities sharply defined), the pinpointing of responsibilities and a whole lot of mutually applied peer pressure resulted in effective step-ups in tempo, to the point where the organizations were advised to hold off on further program implementation. Their ability to get so much out of the program without going the whole route is a tribute to top managements' personal involvements and strongly communicated continuing interests in their organizations' tempos and to the cohesiveness and entrepreneurial spirit of the management teams they've built. In both cases, a tempo test was first administered, with the results conscientiously translated into better delegation, less restrictive corporate procedures and policies, and, of course, job description rewrites.

That's what's been happening when the program works. But as we noted, it didn't work in three organizations, and to know what can go wrong is to go a long way in anticipating potential pitfalls.

If we had to zero in on one basic reason for failure, it would be the failure of top management to make a firm commitment. If top management doesn't take the program seriously, obviously, neither will anyone else. For example, if the VP of Whatever wants to keep his hand on certain areas that bother him, the program's flexibility permits him to assign himself as a second approval authority, or if he's unhappy with a DCA he can reassign that person's responsibility to someone else. But if he's too impatient and starts to make decisions that should be made initially by DCAs at lower levels, he's pretty much put the whammy on the program by introducing confusion and uncertainty into a program designed to eliminate confusion and uncertainty.

Specifically, in one case, the program was instituted at the behest of the chairman–president (and chief executive officer). The executive VP (and chief operating officer) was reluctant to let go of the detail he was used to handling and assigned himself to an inordinate and unnecessary number of decision areas as the second AA. This was bad enough, but he then compounded the problem by blithely ignoring the concomitant responsibility to meet due dates for those decisions. The program obviously could do nothing but fail as everyone gradually lost the incentive to make it work.

In another case, the president appointed his assistant as the decision program manager. Likable, warm, everybody's friend, the type of guy who volunteers to wear the funny apron and help cook the hamburgers at the company's annual picnic, he lacked the tough smarts to keep the program from getting away from him. When a due date was missed, he would smile, pat the offender on the back, and tell him, "Better luck next time." Finally, when his patting arm got tired, he just accepted more and more missed due dates with complete and maddening equanimity. One doesn't have to be an honor student to predict where this program ended up.

In the case of the third company, a turnaround situation (which never did get turned around), DCAs and AAs were kept in their slots long after their inability to handle their share of the program became visible (as it did almost at once). (The program was instituted without a tempo test, which might have forewarned everybody.) These people had never made much of a contribution, but in the absence of previous pressure to get more things done, their individual anonymity had been preserved and this collective incompetence showed up only on the bottom line. When the program brought these individual incompetencies into sharp focus, a benevolent president (who inherited both the job and his ownership from his old dad, who used to cover organizational incompetence by doing the work of 12 men, one mule, and three camels) couldn't bring himself to take the obviously needed steps. He found it easier to fire the program.

INSTITUTING AN MBD PROGRAM

Certain guidelines should be followed in setting up a successful MBD program:

1. In general, top management must make a full-fledged commitment. Beyond this, the selection of the DPM should be made early on so he can become familiar with the program's nuances, help attune its application to the organization's personality, spot any problems that may be lurking below the surface, and better understand the attitudes of its participants.

Ideally, he must be smart, tough, thick skinned, diplomatic, reasonable, and not overbearing or arrogant. He must be prepared to inspire, guide, occasionally kick butts, and watch for slow-tempo pockets. He must convey the impression that he is part of the effort to make the program work, not some remote deity standing on a distant mountaintop dispassionately casting forth an occasional lightning bolt. (Where you find this ideal, I have no idea. It's a pretty good bet that you're going to have to settle for something a whole lot less grandiose. The ones I've seen who make their programs work bleed when you stick them with a pin just like anyone else, but they generally are intelligent and have a pretty realistic grasp of how organizations work and considerable dedication to the program.)

Whoever the DPM is, he must have the backing of top management and his efforts must be periodically reviewed to make sure he's doing his job in a firm but nondisruptive way and that the program is producing the results it set out to achieve.

2. Each participant must not only understand the program, the responsibilities it involves, and the opportunities it presents but should be consulted on what responsibilities he thinks he can handle. One effective way to do this is for the DPM to have each manager on a department-by-department basis, starting at the bottom level, detail what decision areas he is presently responsible for and what decision areas he thinks he can handle as a DCA. The DPM then takes the list to the next upward level for approval or change. Executives at this higher level also check those decision areas for which they want to retain approval authority. They then specify what DCA responsibilities they want to handle, and their list goes to the next level up, and so on. This gives everyone a hand in developing the program, which leads to a better understanding of it and a stronger feeling of participation. ("This is *our* program. Let's make it work," not "This is *their* program. Where's the hooker?")

3. MBD job descriptions should be detailed, published, and constantly updated to avoid confusion.

4. A key point: The organization, from top to bottom, must

accept a whole new level of expectancies in terms of faster decision making, greater individual responsibilities, and a tolerance of some honest mistakes in decision judgment that comes from a higher measure of entrepreneurial responsibility. These expectancies and the opportunities they present for visible individual contribution must be communicated by top management and the DPM so there is no misunderstanding.

5. It goes without saying that top management must be prepared to reward individual effort. One of the virtues of MBD is that it does provide for greater visibility of individual decision making and contribution. Visibility, however, doesn't mean much unless there is some reward (or "punishment"). These rewards can come in the form of promotion, pay raise, additional DCA or AA responsibilities leading to bigger and better things, or a pat on the head. The real sense of individual fulfillment and accomplishment that MBD provides the opportunities for comes only when someone else says in effect, "Atta boy. You did it!"

MBD—A FINAL PERSPECTIVE

MBD, despite its successes, represents a relatively new concept. In time, no doubt, shifts in techniques and emphasis will take place as adjustments are made for organizational differences and as new patterns of higher expectations and new takeoff points settle in. Some of these adaptations are already taking place. But its objectives of stepped-up tempo and greater individual creative participation will *not* change.

It is not my purpose in this chapter to tout MBD. I'm both realistic and cynical enough to recognize that, while it is a fresh approach (with clearly defined objectives) to old problems, it is not the last word. Perhaps it represents only the first step. I hope and expect so. Rather, my objective is to emphasize that present tempo and levels of expectation within our organizations is not something we simply have to accept because our present decision-making process system is engraved in the stone of tradition and precedent. It is my purpose to illustrate the principle that any manager with organizational responsibility is limited only by his imagination in changing the present system to achieve a faster moving, more responsive, more creative organization.

CHAPTER 8

Talk Is Cheap
(Don't You Believe It!)

Many years ago, I had occasion to spend a day working with a jobber salesman, an older, very distinguished man who had until recently been a high school math teacher and whose employer I had just set up as a local distributor for a line of truck batteries. I briefed him on our product, why it was the best in the world, and why it would be sheer insanity for any truck fleet not to buy it. He diligently took notes, which he pored over at lunch. (Right there, I should have suspected trouble.) We made several calls, during which I demonstrated the selling technique that I had found to be very successful. (Translation: No one threw a wrench at us.) Now I came to the biggie—the second largest fleet in the area. "You handle this one," I suggested.

Sailing right in, he extolled the virtues of the product, ranking it two and a half steps above the Colossus of Rhodes as one of the world's great wonders. I sat enraptured as he wove each feature into a magnificent verbal tapestry, building to climactic heights, descending to dramatic pauses, pouring more emotion and feeling into it than Brutus when he tried to explain to the locals why he had stuck it to old Caesar, the people's friend.

Taking advantage of what seemed to be a particularly effective pause that followed one of his many rhetorical questions, the prospective customer cleared his throat, looked at his watch.

"Thanks very much for stopping by," he said in a tone of un-mistakable and unarguable finality. "I'll get back to you."

Outside, I suggested to my gentle, distinguished colleague that he wait in the car. I went back to see the prospect. "What went wrong?" I asked. After some hesitation, he explained, "If I buy from your friend, I'll be on his regular call list. He'll be out to see me at least once a week, pushing his other lines. It took him a half hour to tell me you've got a good product. I believe it. I believed it after the first five minutes, but how can you tell a fine gentleman like that to shut up? My job is to keep a couple of thousand pieces of equipment on the road. If he's going to eat up a half hour or more of my time every time he comes out here, much as I would like to, I just can't afford the time to do business with him."

He had a point.

People talk. We talk. You talk. They talk. Even dolphins talk. Talk, talk, talk. Yak, yak, yak. Ever wonder how much?

I did. And in one of those undertakings that you look back on, scratch your head, and wonder, "Why the hell did I do that?" I set out to find out.

Stopwatch in hand, I analyzed the talking and listening hab-its of 18 executives in 14 companies and came up with some rather startling conclusions.

Our average executive spent an average of six and a half hours a day talking and listening, including meetings, phone conversations, and dictation. Of this six and a half hours, about two and a half were wasted in "conversational fat," which I've defined as that part of a conversation that is not directly re-lated or even relevant to a subject deemed to be important at that moment.

Show me an executive who doesn't chronically complain, "There's just not enough time in the day to get everything done," and I'll show you a guy who pooped out last week. Some make time at the expense of home and family by working 10–12 hours a day. Others accommodate to the barriers imposed by time by simply limiting their output. Yet consider this: Two and half hours of conversational fat placed end to end equals fifteen and a half 40-hour weeks per year! That's *weeks*, dear reader.

If that doesn't jolt you, try this one. If an organization has 100 executives, conversational fat is costing that organization the productive equivalent of about 31 executives. That's 31 percent of an organization's most important and very expensive asset going up in hot air!

WHAT IS CONVERSATIONAL FAT?

Conversational fat is not a nebulous concept but has, in fact, shape, form, and quality—and a whole lot more impact on an organization than we think. For shape and form, it breaks down neatly into four categories:

1. Completely extraneous conversation.
2. Gratuitous background information.
3. Tangential diversion.
4. Conclusion support

While all these are generally woven into most conversations, we can segregate them for purposes of illustration.

Completely extraneous conversation is the easiest to spot because it bears no relevance to business at all. "Guess who I met in Chicago last week?" followed by how they met, where they went for a convivial drink to review old times, what old what's-his-name is doing now, and so forth. Or, "That's a nice looking suit. Where'd you get it?" followed by the source, price, fabric, and who else carries nice suits. Toss in office gossip, last weekend's golf scores, the short story before a meeting that leads to other short stories by those who don't want to be topped in the short story department and this can tie up maybe five or six people for a total lost of two or three man-hours. You get the picture?

Gratuitous background information is often quite interesting, but it's still nonessential and wasteful. The marketing VP between subjects in a marketing review meeting offhandedly asks the sales manager, "By the way, is the Jones order settled yet?" The sales manager grimaces at the thought of all that the Jones people are putting him through. But this is his baby and his opportunity to show how difficult it is to get large accounts and how resourceful and persistent he has to be to do so. So he reviews the last meeting he had with Jones—what happened, where it happened, who said what and how he countered who said what, and where they went to lunch to continue the discussion. From that meeting, he may work back to a few previous meetings to trace the roots of the problems he's had to work out and how the Jones people have been nothing but inconsistent throughout. He may throw in his assessment of Jones's miserable personality and how he's had to contend with the inclination of Jones's assistant to give the order to a competitor, hinting darkly that the assistant must be getting paid off—and on and on.

Tangential diversion is particularly insidious because one subject flows so easily into another. The end of one statement becomes the lead-in for the next. And while all or most of it can somehow relate to business, it is *not* the business at hand.

A production manager asks a subordinate, "Do we have room for this equipment if we decide to buy it?" The answer can be, "No, but we can make room by junking those old dinkers we have on the line that we're not using and never will again." That's a direct response to the question, and if the production manager buys it, fine, they can go on to discussing something else. But often the conversation will become a more detailed discussion of the equipment to be junked, how effective it was when they first bought it (before the subordinate's time), the original cost and what it would cost now if bought new, inflationary costs in general, which leads to a discussion of how the subordinate's Uncle Herbert (that sly old fox) just sold some farmland he bought for $20 an acre 40 years ago for $12,000 an acre to a city slicker developer who's going to load it with condominiums, followed by a discussion of the high price of housing in Duluth, where the production manager might get transferred, to a long discussion of the politics involved in the transfer. . . . Unless the chain is broken by a phone call or they decide it's lunchtime, the tangential conversation can go on forever.

Conclusion support occurs when someone either starts with a conclusion and works back to how that conclusion was reached or worse, starts with the details that led to the conclusion, while all the time keeping the conclusion maddeningly suspended until the very end. All this becomes conversational fat when only the conclusion itself is needed or asked for.

The president asks his VP of marketing, "What are we projecting for the sales of our new line of widgets next year?"

"Two million," replies the VP. That's the conclusion—a direct response to the question. The inclination of many executives, however, would be to deal with the conclusion *and* how the figures were reached—how the market study was done, what interpretations he placed on certain inputs, what people he consulted, and generally how he put the whole thing together. Everything except the conclusion itself is conclusion support—interesting to the listener (maybe) and self-gratifying to the speaker (certainly), but not really essential to the answer. We can assume that if the president questioned the conclusion, he would have asked for its basis.

Although we've broken conversational fat down into categories, remember that the introduction of one type of conversational fat into a conversation opens the door to all the others, and therein lies the opportunity for real time wastage.

WHY DO EXECUTIVES TALK TOO MUCH?

First of all, most executives are pretty voluble and enjoy the give and take of conversation—especially the give. Further, most of us harbor the nagging feeling that we know a whole lot more than we're being given credit for, and what better way to expose others to this little-known fact than by giving verbal expression to this cavernous well of knowledge. Toss in a reluctance to get back to work or come to grips with an unpleasant task ahead, or the need to build up some self-assurance by being listened to. . . .

In fact, the propensity toward conversational fat often reflects an organizational climate in which no one is in a big hurry to get back to work. Witness the guy who, during the course of a normal business day, can piddle away an hour of his and someone else's time in conversational fat. But take the same guy who now has a plane to catch or a dinner party to go to and who is running late. Facing this fast-approaching deadline, he talks faster, cuts right to the heart of matters, shows impatience with peripheral conversation, barks out precise orders, and often makes decisions while shoveling papers into his briefcase that ordinarily would take hours or days to make. Too bad he doesn't always have a plane to catch or a dinner party to go to.

Then there's the phenomenon of "job-time justification," the urge most of us have to justify an expenditure of time. For example, it would be very difficult for the VP of marketing when asked how many widgets he intends to sell during the coming year to respond with an answer that takes less than two seconds to verbalize and not to justify the two or three months of his effort that went into developing that answer and to review the planning that he's done in response to the results of the market study. The only means open to him is to explain what took place during this period of time.

Ask a foreman when a machine will be repaired, and you might get a lengthy blow-by-blow description of what went wrong with it, who screwed it up, and what has to be done to fix it. Often only after he's justified the time it will take will you get the answer you asked for in the first place.

HOW IMPORTANT IS CONVERSATIONAL FAT?

An obvious question at this point is "How important is this whole business of conversational fat? After all, people have been talking forever and will likely continue to do so. Do we have a classic mountain from molehill situation here?"

Anything but. If a person is looking to get the most possible out of an organization (or even to make himself more productive), he can't overlook the sheer waste of potentially productive time conversational fat represents. Ten or 15 weeks a year of lost productive time is 10 or 15 weeks any way you slice it, and this kind of time is a pretty big mountain.

What misleads us is that, taken piece by piece, fat-laden conversation by fat-laden conversation, no single one is going to lessen the effectiveness of an organization or visibly slow its tempo, and this is what makes conversational fat so insidious. Patterns of excessive conversational fat become woven into the personality of an organization and tend to be reflective of the attitude of its people toward getting things done and, to a very large extent, also contribute to that attitude.

Terser, shorter conversational patterns, on the other hand, form one of the climate bases for faster tempo. The leaner these patterns, the faster the tempo tends to be. The faster the tempo, the leaner these patterns *have* to be. Which comes first, the chicken or the egg? We don't know, but there is little question about the interrelationship between tempo and conversational patterns.

SENSING THE DIFFERENCE

In fact, so close is this relationship that I've found that a person can develop a pretty accurate sensitivity to an organization's tempo once exposed to its conversational patterns. Let's assume you're visiting an organization to present it with an idea you're selling. In a fast-tempoed company, chances are the person you're meeting with will ask straight out what you have to offer, indulging only in enough amenities to be polite. If the conversation strays from the reason you're there, he'll probably tolerate it for a few moments while crossing and uncrossing his legs in a negative body language response to your errancy. Then with some impatience in his tone, he'll put you back on the trolley. If you take too long in developing a point, he'll probably push you along by asking specific and pointed questions. If someone walks in to ask your man a question, both the question and the answer will most likely be short and concise. The interview will tend to end abruptly, and any follow-up will be quickly and precisely defined. In short, you will get the feeling that these people have a lot to do, know what they're doing, and are anxious to get to doing it.

Now assume you make the same presentation to a slow-tempoed company. Before getting a chance to develop your message, you'll probably exchange job backgrounds, discover a common interest in basket weaving, and no, you didn't have any trouble finding their place. If someone comes in with a question, you'll probably exchange a little chitchat and perhaps some unimportant background information relative to the question and answer. Meanwhile, your presentation will not come out as tight as you had planned, because it gets bloated around the edges with a lot of conversational fat, a good part of which was introduced by the other guy's interruptions with peripheral questions and observations. In a fast-tempoed organization, questions designed to flesh out what you have to offer are generally reserved until someone determines that there's a basic interest in it. In a slow-tempoed one, the whole picture may be developed and commented on even beyond the point where people know they're not really interested.

CONVERSATIONAL FAT IN PERSPECTIVE

Now that we've exposed, identified, and pummeled conversational fat into a shapeless mass, let's come around 180° and tune into the realities of organizational life. The fact is conversation in an organization is not unlike a piece of steak. A good piece is well marbled with enough fat to give it flavor and tenderness. Too little fat and it tends to be flat and tasteless. Too much and it tends to be gristly, tough, and useless.

With this clever analogy in mind, it is appropriate at this point to concede that conversational fat obviously has some pluses. First of all, it's relaxing. If we had to spend every business day going about like well-programmed automatons speaking only in clipped monotones without a little relaxing banter or gossip, most of us would end up as candidates for that little house in Funny Valley. If the organizational climate didn't get tense under those conditions, it certainly would get boring. And bored or tense people are usually about as useful as snowshoes in July.

Second, a little fat provides for both the expression and development of important nuances that might not otherwise surface. Few things are either all white or all black, and the shadings of gray often emerge in the peripheral or fatty parts of conversations. Third, it helps weld an organization together by helping people within the organization get to know and understand each other better (which could conceivably be a big minus in some cases), as well as helping them be more sensitive to the ebb and flow of organizational currents swirling around them. Finally, and by no means the least important, chance remarks popping up in some fatty conversations often serve to stimulate ideas.

NOW WHAT?

So there you have the pluses and minuses of conversational fat. As with the steak, the realistic, attainable optimum falls somewhere in the middle. What steps, then, can be taken to reach out for this middle ground? No organization I've ever seen needs to add fat to its conversations to achieve the right balance. Therefore, we'll confine our suggestions to the *reduction* of fat. This is a whole lot easier said than done because, until such time as people are cloned with off and on switches, there are no pat formulas to control conversational patterns. There are, however, three steps that can be taken to help shape them.

The first is awareness. Until people are made aware that conversational fat is not a vague concept but in fact real enough to be categorized into four readily recognizable and understandable groups, until they are made aware in the most dramatic terms of what it can cost in time, and until they are made aware that conversational patterns laced with too much fat simply cannot create either the productive time availability or the tone for a fast-tempoed environment, there's little anyone will or can do about it. Awareness provides the perspective, hopefully the incentive, and certainly the starting point.

Let's take a closer look at this relationship between tempo and conversational fat. A fire detector manufacturer had four people in its purchasing department, a purchasing agent and three buyers. The purchasing agent had been with the company since its inception (13 years). Universally liked and respected, he was one of those rare people, of whom there aren't enough in the world, who had the knack of making everyone who walked into his office leave feeling better. Interested in people in general and able to empathize with everyone, he never hurried a salesman. His departmental colleagues, all of whom he had hired, instinctively took their cue from him.

The department developed its own unique conversational pattern. The give-and-take between salesman and buyer was generally relaxed, and the conversation wandered all over the place. Most salesmen cooperated in the talking game, feeling that the long time spent with the buyer was indicative that they were scoring points. Two-hour salesman–buyer lunches were the norm.

There was nothing in the behavior of the department to flag top management's attention. It got its job done, and done well, and the unpaid overtime that individual buyers put in from time to time was accepted as evidence of both their diligence and the scope of their work load. However, at the same time the company was looking into its corporate tempo situation, the purchasing agent submitted a budget request for a fifth man. Bad timing.

The company decided to take a closer look. A rough breakdown of the department's work load and a check of the lobby log sheets, which recorded visitors' time in and time out, turned up too little of the first and too much of the second.

As a result, top management was encouraged to set a couple of new ground rules. Salesmen's visits were to be limited to 20 minutes each, and exceptions were made only in those cases of proven necessity or when a third party had to be called in or a plant tour was in order. Lunches were to be limited to one hour. When the dust cleared and the predictable mumbled reactions were over ("We're being treated like little children. Are we running a business or a kindergarten?"), the department was down to two people doing the same job that four had done—and the company pocketed about $43,000 in saved salaries (more, if you count the requested fifth man). Unfortunately, the company had to accept, with genuine reluctance, the voluntary resignation of the purchasing agent.

In short, the pattern of excessive conversational fat was symptomatic of an overall attitude, a reflection of the slow tempo the department had gotten itself into without anyone really being aware of what was happening. The company could have come in from one direction and licked it by firing one or two people and distributing their work loads to the survivors on an "or else" basis. Instead it opted to come in from the other direction and assault the *conversational time frames* in which this slow tempo flourished. If nothing else, the existence of this option indicates the close relationship between tempo and conversational patterns. Again, which is cause and which is effect, we'll leave to you, dear reader, to sort out. Probably the answer is, either one and both.

As a prelude to Step 2, let's stress again that there is nothing wrong with a little banter to keep the atmosphere light, friendly, and relaxing or even to lighten up a point you wish to make without coming on too strong or combatively. Not only is it not wrong, it can be very right.

But time, place, and moderation all play a role in making it useful, which brings us to the most insidious effect of conversational fat, aside from time wastage and its effect on tempo—its distractive effect on concentration. Get a group together (or even a couple of people), zero in on a problem, concentrate on *it* and nothing else, develop some momentum, and chances are that a solution, good or bad, will be found. But lace the same situation with liberal doses of conversational fat, periodically rechanneling everyone's concentration off into 10 other directions, and the problem focus will be lost. When attempts are made to refocus, they often don't quite hit the same target or develop the same momentum, and this is one reason why so many meetings and discussions seem to go on interminably and end up indecisively. When this occurs systemically throughout the organization, the impact on the organization's ability to function tightly is obviously impaired.

The solution (Step 2): Where possible, segregate these digressions so they don't intrude on problem-solving meetings, unless at some point a break is desirable to clear some brains before resuming an attack on a particularly vexatious problem.

A business machine manufacturer had a pattern of long indecisive meetings. Their inability to reach quick decisions and solutions was ascribed to the difficult nature of the problems themselves. The president was one of the 18 who had participated in my research, and part of the deal was that I would make him privy to the results. I sat in on one of his weekly department head meetings and stopwatched the fat at about 60 percent. Both impressed and dismayed, he had his secretary record, in shorthand, the next meeting. When he reviewed the typed notes, he concluded that close to 50 percent was fat. (Little wonder indecision was the usual end product.) The problem went undetected previously simply because no one thought there was anything abnormal in their mode of communicating at meetings—and by most standards, there wasn't.

The president solved the problem quite simply. First he lectured the troops on conversational fat, its four categories and what it cost in wasted weeks per year. (He shot gloriously from the hip on this one. With no firm basis other than he now knew his organization talked too much, he announced loftily that they were piddling away time in conversational fat at the rate of 21 weeks per year. Even I raised an eyebrow. But he was the president, and if he said "21 weeks," then dammit, it was 21 weeks!)

He had a blackboard mounted in the conference room. On one side he listed permanently the four categories of conversational fat, and on the other he chalked in the subject of the meeting, or if new subjects came up during the meeting, he would chalk them in as they came up. Pointing to the subject to be discussed, he started with, "This is all we'll talk about until we resolve it." If he noticed the conversation straying into one of the four conversational fat categories, he would swivel around and point to the appropriate category. "You're over here, Englebert," he would chide icily. "Let's get back here," pointing to the subject matter on the other side.

The first meeting was replete with er-ing and ah-ing and dead silences. Patterns are not easy to break. But by the third meeting, a new tone had firmly taken root. Not only did the tenor of the meetings become more incisive, but the meetings which had been scheduled from 8:30 to noon, now generally broke up by 10:00. More got done in less time by pruning the distractive fat from their conversation.

Carried away with new-found enthusiasm, the president had a two-way sign placed on each executive's desk—one side facing the executive, the other facing outward. Both sides carried the same message, "Stick to the point, dammit!" Because most of the department heads who participated in staff meetings saw firsthand the fruits of sticking to the point, they supported the intent of the sign by infusing this awareness among their subordinates. Although it can't be measured, there is general agreement that the change in conversational patterns and its results in terms of more productive movement and more incisiveness, especially among middle management, have taken on dramatic dimensions.

The third step in fat reduction is to keep people busy enough so that tighter conversational patterns become necessary in order to get done what they have to get, or ought to get, done. We won't dwell on this, because this is what the second part of this book was all about and we've just about said it all.

As noted, some fat is good; too much is no good. But look

at it this way: If my research is representative of conditions that exist in most businesses, and I have no reason to believe it isn't, then even a 50 percent reduction in conversational fat means that an executive team can pick up another seven to eight weeks of productive time a year. And that, as the man says, ain't hay.

PART THREE

THE KEY TO
REACTING POSITIVELY

Positive and Negative Orientations

The birth, demise, and rebirth of a new idea—or, class will tell. A true story.

Chapter 1. Several years ago, a toy and game company that sells primarily to toy and game shops, department stores, and higher quality discounters held one of its periodic "new product review" meetings, the purpose of which was to review new products developed by its R&D department.

Out of the 13 or 14 presented, 3 products were discarded as being "too supermarketish," a company euphemism for too cheap and unsophisticated. A junior marketing assistant who was an official liaison between marketing and R&D and never quite understood what his duties were other than to go for coffee for both groups made a suggestion. "That's what we said at our last meeting when we threw some products out. Why don't we put them all together into a line specifically for supermarkets? Their development costs are mostly behind us, and supermarkets are a whole new area of action."

Three marketing people pointedly ignored the intrusion. Another, a product line manager, replied archly that this was not their market, and when Junior had a few more years experience under his belt, he would come to understand that. "You can't serve two masters," said the product line manager.

Junior Marketing Assistant persisted, "It would pose no hardship on our production facilities. All we'd have to do is develop a marketing adjunct to sell it."

The product manager sighed. "The markets are different," he explained with that exaggerated forebearance that some people maddeningly use to emphasize someone else's stupidity. "The pricing structure is different. The selling techniques are different. The servicing requirements are different. You can't serve two masters."

There we go again thought the junior marketing assistant. He was unconvinced, but before he could express his lack of conviction, someone suggested with an exaggerated sigh of futility, "Let's break for lunch." At that moment Junior Marketing Assistant made a decision.

Chapter 2. Two years later, the company, finding itself in financial trouble because of competition from other larger more aggressive toy and game manufacturers, sold out to a chemical manufacturer. The chemical manufacturer tried it for 18 months, pumped more money in, pumped some old executives out, and finally decided it had better stick to chemicals.

Junior Marketing Assistant had left the company shortly after the fateful meeting, borrowed $40,000 from an indulgent father-in-law and another $20,000 from his friendly banker, appropriated some of the lines his old employer had rejected, and went into the business of supplying supermarkets with toys. In an ironic twist of fate, tucked away in a 3-man marketing group that works for him is his former colleague who had suggested they break for lunch on that fateful day. Junior Marketing Assistant, now Successful Junior Marketing Tycoon, has never mentioned the incident.

Noblesse oblige.

In the section on tempo, we noted several times that organizations move only by making decisions. Taking this a step further, we can add that organizations move *ahead* only by making decisions relative to *new* ideas and that every one of these new ideas is fed into a network of orientations that are different for each organization. Some are specific, influenced by the organization's perception of its goal. For example, the toy and game company discussed above saw its purpose in life as being to develop new, bigger, and better toys and games for the market it knew, not to develop new, bigger, and perhaps better markets. When Junior Marketing Assistant proposed a new approach, it was almost preordained that the suggestion would be shunted along the pathway to oblivion.

Orientations (or predispositions), however, go beyond the specific. They also exist as pervasive climates, giving organizations overall inclinations toward negativism or positivism. To put it another way, predispositions toward new ideas are either positively or negatively charged, and most organizations are by nature somewhat negatively charged.

This inclination toward negativism is created in part by the comforting sense that not adopting a new idea (which starts with not considering it seriously) preserves the status quo, and seemingly carries with it little or no perceptible *immediate* risk. This propensity toward a negative orientation is not unlike body muscle tone. Even in a relaxed state, it's always there. As a result, there is generally more negativism toward new ideas than we recognize. It can kill the full growth potential of an organization, and if pronounced, can kill the organization along with the potential.

Yet, despite the importance of these orientations, we generally tend to ignore their existence. A new idea gets introduced into our organization. It's accepted or rejected. That's it. We never stop to think that maybe the *inclination* to accept or reject the idea, for all the right or wrong reasons, was in place long before the idea was introduced. That is "orientational myopia." And the purpose of this chapter is to strip away the blinders and focus on recognizing, defining, and identifying these positive and negative orientations.

POSITIVE AND NEGATIVE ORIENTATIONS IN ACTION

Let's start this process of recognition by using as an example two companies facing the same situation. For purposes of illustration, we'll revert to our old example of a proposed purchase of a new piece of equipment and express the contrast in the extremes, with no gray shadings, with our simple all-good-guys-wear-white-hats and all-bad-guys-wear-black-hats approach:

Company A: At an interdepartmental meeting, Roger, an engineer, suggests they buy a new piece of equipment he's been looking into. "It's a honey," says Roger. "It will outproduce our present equipment by 10 percent, giving us a higher rate of production and a lower unit cost. And its price is only $100,000."

"Only $100,000!" snorts Finance. "Do you have any idea what the carrying charge is on $100,000 today? At today's rates, there's no such a thing as *only* $100,000!"

Production pipes up. "We don't have room for another paper clip, let alone a new piece of capital equipment. Besides, this equipment calls for different operating techniques, and retraining our people will be costly, time consuming, and disruptive. Putting in new equipment at this time would tear us to pieces."

Sales senses trouble. This could put him under the gun, so he hastens to head it off at the pass. "What good is more production if we're going to have a problem selling it? We didn't invent this economy, but with the way things are now, our problem is selling what we're making, not adding production."

Now let's take the same situation at Company B. That company's Roger makes the same presentation. Finance tweaks his nose thoughtfully, whips out his old hand calculator, makes a few calculations, and suggests, "If we drop our unit costs by even 5 percent, we can achieve a pay-back in 18 months. Money is tight and costly, but for this kind of opportunity, we could find it somewhere."

Production adds, "It would take room we don't now have. We'd have to add 10,000 feet by cutting through the north wall and building an addition. That would cost a buck or two, but if we could add that much production at a lower cost, it might figure out to be worth the investment. We'd have to phase in a retraining program, but if we started early enough and got some help from the equipment manufacturer, that shouldn't be too big a problem.

Sales pops up, "Hey, if it really worked out to a 5 percent cost reduction, that could be just what I need. We could drop our prices 5 percent and by increasing our sales make it back on a lower per unit overhead cost. Meanwhile, we'll cream the competition. This might be just the edge I've been looking for in this tight market."

Whether the case has been made for or against the purchase, an argument can be made for each position expressed. In deference to Company A, money is expensive, no question about it. Room is tight. An obvious fact. The economy is creating a tough market to sell in. Indisputable. Even so, the distinction between the two companies is strikingly clear.

Company A is negatively oriented. The thrust of its reaction is to view the new idea negatively as a *risk*. Company B is positively oriented. The thrust of its reaction is to view the new idea positively as an *opportunity*.

Company A overviews the new idea in terms of the *problems* implementation would create. Company B overviews it in terms of the *solutions* to those problems.

Company A *stops* thinking creatively with the problems. Company B *starts* thinking creatively with the problems.

And that, dear reader, is essentially what positive and negative orientations are all about.

WHERE YOU FIND NEGATIVE ORIENTATION

Negative orientation can be found anywhere at any level of management. You may argue, not without justification, that most top managers didn't get to the top by saying "no" as an automatic reflex or by looking at bright new opportunities through smoked glasses and that therefore negative orientation doesn't usually occur at that level. T'ain't so. For example:

A financial man is elevated to top management. He may be hell on wheels when it comes to raising and handling money, putting together intricate acquisition deals, instituting tight budgetary controls, and understanding the often strange variabilities of costs. But hit him with a new marketing concept that involves not only the science of numbers but the art of evaluating marketing risk as well and, from his vantage point and frames of reference (in other words, his predisposition or orientation), he may see all kinds of risks and problems instead of opportunities.

Orientations at top levels can change. A company founder can invest a good part of his life in building his organization. He's perhaps developed a standard of living and a reputation for success that he becomes increasingly protective of, and he may become more and more leery of new ideas that, because of inherent risks, may jeopardize what he's managed to accumulate.

An executive who has climbed up close to the top can suddenly feel the hot breath of a competitor on the back of his neck for the next spot and as a result concentrates more and more of his efforts on avoiding that one fatal mistake that could tilt the race in favor of the other guy. And accepting or endorsing a new idea could be just that mistake.

At top levels negative orientation, like slow tempo, often becomes apparent because of its impact on the bottom line, loss of market position, and the like. It is usually less apparent at lower levels, and this makes it more insidious there. Individual effects tend to be smaller than at top levels, but the total cumulative effect of negative orientation at lower levels can be just as far reaching.

For example, policies, projects, and organizational directions established at top levels are generally fleshed out and implemented at lower levels. If these policies are executed with little imagination and innovation, the end product is not always going to be what was originally envisioned. And this is exactly what happens when they're fed into a negatively oriented climate. Even worse, it's impossible to count the number of opportunities a company loses because the ideas were introduced into the organization at lower-level pockets of negative orientation, found nothing to cling to, and simply disappeared.

Overall, negative orientation—of individuals, of segments of an organization, or of the organization as a whole—tends to dry up creative juices, encouraging the organization or part of it to function statically, routinely, and mechanically, not aggressively, creatively, and with a forward thrust.

ORIENTATION INFLUENCES

Orientations are influenced by many factors. Some are external. A company in the garment business, which often must turn on a dime, which lives (and probably thrives) in a world of cutthroat competition, which historically spends little on functional R&D, which spends half its energies actively wooing and entertaining buyers, is oriented differently toward new ideas than a manufacturer of, say, sophisticated medical equipment, which spends most of its energies on functional R&D and moves slowly because each product innovation is expensive and time consuming, and whose selling is done in passionless dignity by engineers to scientists.

The stage of a company's development affects its orientation. A very young, freewheeling company with a hot new product and a shoestring to work on—whose every move sets a new precedent—is going to look at new ideas differently than a more mature company with more fixed and rigid operating procedures, operating in a more predictably competitive environment.

A rural southern mattress maker in a modern new plant probably has a different orientation toward new ideas than an older urban New England company in an older, more cramped converted mill building making the same product. The first is likely to be oriented toward growth, the other toward survival. Their reception of new ideas is related to these goals.

Equally important are internal influences on orientation. A company with an aggressive top management whose personality and drive are such that it demands constant recognition and is looking to conquer the world has a different orientation from a company whose top management is chiefly concerned with developing a growth pattern in a more patient and orderly cost-conscious way.

A history of success or failure influences an organization's level of confidence and with it its propensity for risk taking and thus its orientation toward new ideas. A company whose people have unique problem-solving skills is less afraid to tackle and develop new ideas than one whose people are less skilled.

THE STRUCTURE OF POSITIVE AND NEGATIVE ORIENTATIONS

Orientations, as noted, can't be quantified. But fortunately, we do have a device that will put them into a simple, understandable perspective and provide some basis for helping to manage them. But first a word of explanation.

Not every idea is a good one, nor is every one a bad one.

An idea is submitted to a group. Half thinks it's great; half thinks it's terrible. Those who like it point to the others and say, "Aha! See, you're negatively oriented!" "Not so," retort the critics. "We reject it because it lacks merit. It's simply a bad idea."

This tells little of the group's orientation. Both sides may in fact have some pretty sound reasons for their opinions. The key to the group's orientation lies not in whether the idea is perceived as good or bad (we're not concerned here with the merits of the idea) but in where and how it is rejected (we'll use the term *aborted*) or finally accepted. With this in mind, let's now take a look at Exhibit 14.

Negative Orientation

You'll note that on the left-hand side of the exhibit, we've bracketed Steps 1 and 3 only. In a negatively oriented group (and even though we keep referring to a group, all the points we'll discuss apply to individuals as well), that's all the members generally consider, and the idea can be easily aborted at either point.

A common reaction to a new idea in a negatively oriented environment is "instant denigration" (Step 1). For example, old friend Roger suggests buying that same old piece of equipment. Immediately, Herbert says, "Right now we've got bigger problems than that." Jasper adds, "If we have that kind of money, I know a hundred better places to put it." Harold pipes up, "You have no guarantee it'll do what they claim it will." Edgar has to have the last word, "Forget it. There's nothing wrong with our present equipment." (Atta boy, Edgar!)

When they get through, poor Roger is either completely frustrated, madder than hell, or more likely, if the weight of numbers, stronger personalities, or rank are against him, thoroughly subdued. His idea was not really considered on its po-

EXHIBIT 14. How a decision is made—negative versus positive orientation.

Negative Orientation			Positive Orientation
Instant denigration	*	1. Statement of new idea	
		2. Analysis of consensus of potential profitability of new idea	* Evaluation of potential benefits
Emphasis on or magnification of problems and risks	*	3. Analysis or problems and potential risks of implementation	
		4. Development of solutions to problems of implementation and steps to minimize potential risks	* Analysis of solution feasibility and cost of problem-risk solutions
		5. Point of final decision, based on potential benefits of 2 above versus costs of 4 above	* Profitability analysis

*Potential abortion points.

tential merits. Rather, it was instantly denigrated and consigned to oblivion.

There are many ways to instantly denigrate a new idea and effectively kill it. It can be done in terms of organizational problems ("We're too busy for that right now" or "We're simply not geared for it") or in terms of the idea itself ("It'll never work" or "We tried something like that a long time ago and it fell apart"). You can ignore the suggestion and slide the conversation around it, a common technique. You can suggest it be held in abeyance and see to it that time runs out. Even ridicule works ("Is that the best you can come up with?"). One of the most effective instant denigrators I've ever seen in action had a unique method. When an idea was proposed, he would stare at the suggestor in silence for 10 or 20 seconds without expression, then slowly break out in a grin, then a hearty chuckle, and go on to a new subject. (He could get away with it. He was the general manager of a corporate division. The division now has a new general manager.)

Now suppose the idea somehow gets beyond the first step in one piece. Another trap awaits it at Step 3. The technique here is quite simple. Just about every idea has some implementation problems, or it creates other problems. Just about every idea involves some risk. To prove that the idea is unworthy of further consideration, negatively oriented people simply magnify those problems and risks. Jasper notes, "To make room, we'd have to tear the shop apart and disrupt our whole operation." (He comes across as perceptive.) Herbert tosses in, "$100,000 is a hell of a lot of money to risk on a piece of unproven equipment. We could be sitting here with a piece of useless iron on the floor and no money to pay our bills with." (He comes across as fiscally prudent.) Edgar still wants the last word. "And what'll we do with our present equipment, write it off and take a balance sheet beating on it? That's ridiculous." (You tell 'em, Edgar!)

In a negatively oriented group, that's usually it. It has two cracks at aborting the new idea and, with some imagination, both have a pretty good shot at working. This brings us to one of the keys to spotting a negative group (or individuals): In almost every instance, a Step 2 analysis of the potential merits of the new idea is sloughed over! The idea is either wiped out by instant denigration or the emphasis is placed on the problems and risks it involves, but the idea as a potential *opportunity* is seldom seriously or enthusiastically examined.

Another key to identifying negative orientation: When the problems are introduced, little or no attempt is made to find solutions. This is why Step 3 is bracketed alone on the negative side. Obviously, if there has been no serious attempt to develop a Step 2 consensus about potential opportunity, there is no compelling incentive to solve problems of implementation. It's pretty hard to encourage seeking solutions in the absence of any enthusiasm for the idea that would create the problems in the first place.

Positive Orientation

Steps 1 and 2 are bracketed together on the positive side because a positively oriented group tends to view an idea in terms of the potential opportunity it represents. The *initial* reaction to the idea is to isolate it and zero in on what it can or will do for the organization, and at this point the problems of implementation are not usually taken into account—or, indeed, allowed to intrude.

(Going to an extreme, we've all seen this happen: Someone tosses an idea into a highly positively charged group, and the first reaction is excitement, which mounts as everyone vies with everyone else to spot all its potential advantages. Often the advantages get blown out of proportion and some cooler head has to throttle back the enthusiasm and inject some sobering perspective, perhaps saying in effect, "O.K., wait a minute. Let's see what kind of money we're *really* talking about." Or "Whoa, has anyone considered this?")

In a positively oriented group, one of two things can happen at the end of Step 2. The idea can be judged to be no good, in which case it is rejected at that point—on its merits. If, however, the consensus is that it has potential merit, then the positively oriented group will move to Steps 3 and 4 *together*. Because of the enthusiasm and incentive developed in Step 2, problems and risks are now viewed in the context of their possible solutions. Problems are stated not as a device to kill the idea but simply to define the areas for which solutions must be sought. At this point, the original idea may be fine tuned or amended to accommodate to feasible solutions.

Now assume that the group decides that the solutions are not practical or are too costly or that the risks obviously outweigh any potential benefits that can reasonably be expected, then the idea is aborted at the end of Step 4. On the other hand, if the group decides that the solutions make practical sense and that the more obvious risks are manageable, it then moves to Step 5—a closer evaluation of whether the potential benefits outweigh the cost of the proposed solutions and whether these benefits outweigh any risks that must be taken. If so, the idea is in a "go" mode. If not, then Step 5 becomes the final abortion point for a positively oriented group.

In Practice

The steps we've outlined in Exhibit 14 are not always as precise as our illustration suggests. For example, in a negative group, an idea can be both instantly denigrated and the problems magnified in the same sentence, or the reaction can bounce between them. In a positively oriented group, the participants may be so attuned to recognizing potential benefits that a particular new idea may require no conscious Step 2 consensus, and the group may move directly from the statement of the idea right to the problem and problem solution phase.

In some cases, an idea can be construed as so impractical that even a positively oriented group can dismiss it precipitately.

Someone comes up with the brilliant idea that the way to loosen up a tight profit margin is to double prices and thereby quadruple profits. Without the need for much discussion, the group might instantly conclude that doubling prices would result in zero sales. Or let's say Roger's new piece of equipment, delightful as it would be to have in the plant, is simply priced way beyond the capability of the company to pay for it. Such an idea might be instantly rejected by either a positive or negative group. In a mixed group, an idea can carom off the various steps in argument and counterargument.

Some people are slow starters. Perhaps they are poor interpolators. They may sneer initially at an idea, but as it's developed, their enthusiasm may mount. Others are born devil's advocates. They act negatively oriented, not for the purpose of killing the idea necessarily, but to steer the conversation into a probing of possible flaws. Then they turn out to be positively oriented. Some are expert in stating premises so positively that others tend to accept them as fact, especially if the person has a particularly forceful personality. ("Based on the experience of other companies, if we go to a four-day, 10-hours-a-day week, you'd better damn well figure that our production rate will drop at least 10 percent," when in fact he actually has no basis for the premise.) In reading a group's orientation, all these possible deviations must be kept in mind.

The point is that the steps outlined in Exhibit 14 comprise neither a conscious nor absolute procedure. But in the main, I've found, once a person becomes sensitized to catch *initial* reactions and filters them through the steps of Exhibit 14, it doesn't take a whole lot of time before he can pretty much identify the orientation of a group or its individuals. This, of course, is one of the practical applications of Exhibit 14.

Here's another application. This is the story of two company CEOs who recognized a negative orientation problem among their staffs and use Exhibit 14 as a direct working tool. One has it painted on a conference room blackboard. The other has

it mounted on a piece of large poster cardboard on a floor tri-
pod near his desk. The first uses a rolled-up calendar as a
pointer (and occasional back scratcher). When discussing a new
idea and the initial reaction is instant denigration, for example, he'll point to Step 1 on the negative side. "Malcolm," he'll
chide gently with a disarmingly benign smile, "you're here.
Let's get the hell over here [pointing to Step 2, positive side]
and see what we've really got for an idea. Let's not be so damn
quick to ash-can it." If Malcolm pulls too many times to the
negative side, the gentle chiding gets less and less gentle, the
language more expressive. Under the CEO's steady hand and
prodding, his people's approach to new ideas, he's observed
with satisfaction, seems to have made a fairly rapid switch from
the negative side to the positive.

The second CEO is a snuff-sniffing, short, stocky, balding
man who plays a pretty studied role of curmudgeon, I suspect
because he thinks the world expects it of him (and he does a
pretty good job). Not known for his happy-go-lucky approach
to life or his ready wit, he is given to closing his eyes during
meetings. However, lest anyone thinks he's asleep, if he hears
what appears to be a manifestation of negative orientation, he
growls (without opening his eyes) in a low throaty rumble, "I
hear Step 3, left. I want to hear a Step 3–4, right." His people
know that means he's hearing problems on the negative side
when he wants to hear problems *and* solutions together on the
positive side. After four months, when asked how the program was working, he replied with a growl, "I'm growling
less." (I take this to mean his people are thinking more positively—or the snuff is getting to him.)

THE PACKAGED IDEA AND NEGATIVE ORIENTATION

Not every idea is expressed spontaneously. Take a fellow sitting at his desk pondering a problem. Suddenly, the comic

strip light bulb flashes over his head. He has a solution. He develops it, anticipates objections, assesses the likely problems, and makes some cogent risk assessments. He supports his premises with what seem to be solid facts. He's now covered all the five steps in Exhibit 14 and has an idea wrapped up in a complete package.

When confronted with this type of packaged idea, expressions of negative orientation have to be more subtle because of the nature of the presentation. After all, it's pretty hard to instantly denigrate an idea that has touched most of the obvious bases without blatantly exposing your negativism.

Although the thrust of negative orientation can be somewhat blunted by the packaged approach, there are still ways of attacking. The obvious ones are to question the figures, sneer at the premises upon which the idea is based, and take minor problems perhaps overlooked by the presenter and explode them into major potential crises, using these either as a reason to reject the idea or as "proof" that the package is incomplete and thus suspect.

But what does a negatively oriented person do when confronted with an idea that is so tightly packaged that little opportunity is open for this approach? Or what does he do if the proponent is of such rank or represents such a strong will or has marshaled such logic on his side that it becomes something less than prudent to mount a frontal assault? One technique is to listen, smile, nod, and then do nothing to implement, or to make mountains out of implementary molehills, or to drag feet in putting together some of the implementation, hoping that as time passes initial ardor and passions will dim or maybe the idea will be made obsolete by changing conditions. This approach, I've found (and you probably will also if you analyze whatever happened to some good ideas floating around in your organization that somehow never quite made it to shore), is more widespread than commonly appreciated and in the right hands can be pretty effective.

WHAT MAKES PEOPLE NEGATIVELY ORIENTED?

Even though they entwine, overlap, and blend, we can for
purposes of better definition break down the causes of negative orientation into two categories: personal and environmental. First the personal. There are no doubt deep psychological
reasons behind the negative orientation of many individuals.
For our purposes, however, we're less concerned with the fact
that Herbie's mother didn't care a whole hell of a lot for Herbie or that Rudy developed a justifiable paranoia when Mabel
Diddleweather refused his invitation to their high school junior prom and more concerned with a more practical aspect,
namely: A primary basis of negative orientation, especially at
lower management levels, is the desire of those negatively oriented not to have to implement a new idea—and the best way
to avoid that is to abort the idea, the quicker the better.

I have found that most of the reasons that produce a slow
corporate or individual tempo also produce a negative orientation. Take timidity, for example. Timid people are uncomfortable with responsibilities that involve solving problems or
being associated with risks—especially where the possibility
of being held accountable for failure exists (as it does inevitably in most new ventures and projects)—and they'll do their
best to avoid such responsibilities. Timidity is probably the
single greatest cause of negative orientation.

Related to this is incompetence, the inability to solve problems, handle new projects, accommodate to a new procedure,
or take on additional responsibilities. Acceptance of a new idea
could mean facing any or all of these, and what better way to
avoid this firing line exposure than to try to see to it that the
idea never becomes an implementable project. Add another
facet of incompetence: Many people simply lack the imagination or background to absorb the details, nuances, and ramifications of a new idea and wouldn't recognize a good one if
it bonked them on their heads.

Laziness and inertia also contribute to negativism. The executive who sees himself as overworked, often because he has a tempo problem, tends to resist new ideas that may result in adding to his already "overwhelming" work load or that may require changes in his well-rooted work patterns.

The "to hell with it, it's not my idea" syndrome clobbers many new ideas. Some people simply find it difficult to accept anyone else's idea as being a good one. ("If it's such a good idea, I'd have thought of it myself." Or "So-and-So simply doesn't understand the problem as I do.") Or a superior may react to a good idea by a subordinate as a threat. I even met one executive, a business school MBA, who came up with all kinds of negative responses to new ideas except from people whose academic credentials he felt made the idea credible.

Environmentally, there are climates operating within the organization that contribute to a negative orientation. For example, an environment created by weak leadership, amorphous organizational structure, or goal incoherence can encourage factionalism, fierce competition between executives, or personal jealousies or defenses of the departmental fiefdoms that tend to crop up in nearly every organization. This creates antagonisms that encourage negative reactions to the "other side's" ideas or, as likely, make some people not want to contribute their skills, as they might have to if the idea is accepted, to someone else's possible success.

In the environmental department, our old friend slow corporate tempo makes a pretty good contribution. Having to solve problems means that someone has to make decisions or get them approved or wait for someone else to make them. If the process is going to be agonizingly slow and frustrating, many people tend to shy away from new ideas, since trying to get them adopted could thrust them smack in the middle of this frustration. Instead, they feel that their time is better spent on those things over which they have control.

An organizational environment that encourages poor delegation tends to create a negative orientation. If responsibilities are properly delegated to an executive and there's a regular process for evaluating his results, his job can be a source of challenge, satisfaction, and visibility. His responsibility for contributing to a project becomes well defined and meaningful. He has repeated opportunities to sharpen his problem-solving skills, and when people become good problem solvers, they tend to look for opportunities to use these skills. These are the positively oriented.

But when someone is constantly spelling out the "how" for a subordinate—looking over his shoulder, correcting, challenging, and second-guessing—it doesn't take a whole lot of time before the subordinate says, "To hell with it. All I am is an extension of someone else." There's no fulfillment in what he's doing. He can't lay claim to any credit for any ability he might have been able to demonstrate. The job becomes unrewarding, boring, and sometimes tense. To avoid this, he tends to want to nip any new idea in the bud.

Another environmental cause is also one we covered under slow tempo: patterns of long time lapses between decision and implementation. Propose an idea, develop a consensus of enthusiasm and excitement for it, set an immediate date for implementation, assign responsibilities, stand back, and chances are the wheels and gears will spark and turn and mesh and produce. With the details and objectives of the idea and its potential rewards in full fresh view, with the initial enthusiasm and excitement still intact, everybody is full of go-juice and vinegar.

Now take the same idea, develop the same initial enthusiasm and excitement, but instead schedule implementation for way down the road or for the "first chance we get." Stand back and watch the wheels and gears creak, squeak, and grind to a halt. The original enthusiasm has faded into the mist, the excitement has slid down the drainpipe, and suddenly no one can find the time to do anything about the project until someone comes along and either pushes panic buttons or does some all-around butt kicking. (It's always been a source of amazement to me how many enthused and excited people have no trouble finding time for implementing a new project and how these same people, once the fine edge of this enthusiasm and excitement has been dulled by time, can't find any time for it unless they're dragooned into it.)

An organization that's too tightly structured, with layer after layer of approval points through which a new idea must wend before it's finally approved or rejected, creates a remoteness in space and time between someone's creative thinking and the decision point, and this encourages a negative orientation.

A top management that discourages an entrepreneurial spirit among subordinates turns out mechanics, not creative imaginative executives receptive to new ideas. A company philosophy that places as much emphasis on avoiding mistakes as on reaching for a star or two tends to create a negative organizational climate. (It's no secret that it's pretty hard to pin a mistake on anyone who avoids doing anything except taking up space.) And, of course, a conservative organization that looks at every new idea primarily in terms of the money to be risked rather than as an opportunity to make money encourages a negative orientation.

CHAPTER 10

Measuring the Negative— Another Takeoff Point

In the early 1970s, the oil sheiks plugged the free flow of oil. Prices skyrocketed. Near panic hit the Western world.

This is the true story of two custom molding plastics companies operating within this period. Their raw material was petroleum based; their molding processes were based on steam. Oil, therefore, was a big part of their cost structures. By necessity, their raw material suppliers boosted prices with the subtlety and frequency of a chattering machine gun.

Both the molding industry and the raw material suppliers recognized the danger. If they didn't stay competitive with non-oil-intensive materials, they wouldn't have an industry. Unhappily, these non-oil-intensive competitive products lagged behind in cost increases, widening the gulf. Their only salvation—cut costs.

The "how" of it was simple: Reduce raw material usage by sharper product designing, and cut fuel consumption by becoming more fuel efficient. With some desperation, their trade association convened a two-day all-business, no-nonsense technical seminar. In a frenzy of mutual cooperation and goodwill, many molders made some of their cherished manufacturing secrets available. The raw material suppliers with their vast capacity for research outlined new methods. The tools for salvation were there.

The first company's representatives to the conference returned home raring to go. When they sat down to review what they had learned and to determine what they could practically implement, their initial enthusiasm dampened. The requirements for implementation, they suddenly realized, were both costly and strenuous. New molding methods designed to cut steam usage called for considerable outlays of effort and money. They diddled and fussed and found all kinds of "logical" reasons to wait, defer, and temporize. Maybe there were better, less costly ways, they reasoned. It's not too prudent to rush into anything and jeopardize what they had already built before the crunch hit. Mistakes could be very costly . . . and on and on and on.

Then gradually, as their ardor for coming to grips with the problem abated, so did the problem. While costs didn't level off, they began to increase at a much slower rate. Then finally, the oil glut of the early 1980s relieved the pressure entirely. At least this is how they rationalized their failure to act decisively.

Meanwhile, the second company went through the same initial process. Its response was to set up a program to implement many of the new ideas, some of which loomed large on the problem front when first discussed but which became surprisingly less so when reduced to a tightly scheduled program of implementation. While accepting the fact that it couldn't implement all the new techniques, the company did some creative numbers work and considerable belt tightening and set up a program for financing what it felt it could do. Its primary overview of what it learned at the seminar was that this was an *opportunity* to survive, and this provided the incentive to act. The first company had seen only the *risks*, which provided the incentive *not* to act.

Meanwhile, the first company heaved a sigh of relief. It had gotten over the hump in one piece. But then another more subtle crisis arose. While the second company (and several others in the same marketing area) had reduced its energy use, it had simultaneously, by ripple effect, reduced its rate of increasing costs in other areas. Head to head in the marketplace, the first company suddenly found itself priced not only out of the ball game but out of the league. It went phfft.

The president-owner of the now defunct first company became a salesman for a former competitor. He met one of the owners of the second company at a large account for which they were both competing. It was late in the day. They went out for a drink. Three Bloody Marys later, the president of the defunct company lamented his fate. "My guys kept telling me what we couldn't do and why we couldn't do it. After a while, I believed them. I still can't figure it out. I don't think we slipped backward. We just didn't move ahead. Somehow, things just slipped away from us."

"You're right," agreed the owner of the second company sadly. "Things just slipped away." The president of the defunct company didn't hear. "Things just slipped away from us," he echoed into his empty glass.

It wasn't a total loss. The second company owner picked up the check.

This story is a classic illustration of the predictable difference in results between negative and positive orientations. There were few secrets in the industry. Supplier salesmen, trade association meetings, and salesmen job hopping between molders all provided the means for an exchange of information. Both orientations could have been recognized in their early states had the companies used the readily available information to compare their positions with their competitors, and to determine whether they were leaders, followers, or laggards. Invariably, leaders tend to be positively oriented, while followers are somewhat negatively oriented and laggards are flat-out negatively oriented.

IDENTIFYING ORIENTATION

This brings us now to the subject of identification. It starts first with an understanding of Exhibit 14 and how the reaction to new ideas reflects a group's orientation.

In most cases, this process falls right into place. In others, it gets a little slippery because we are dealing with a sometimes imprecise attitude that can shift back and forth. For example, Delbert is generally negatively oriented. He has more "We can'ts" and "We shouldn'ts" and "It won't works" than a stingy squirrel has acorns at first snowfall. But Delbert has a few pet ideas, maybe because of some success he's had with them in the past, and when some variation of these themes is proposed, by either himself or someone else, old Delbert suddenly books first class passage on the good ship "Positive Orientation." Conversely, a person who is generally positively oriented can have a few prejudices in some areas and become Mr. A-1 Negative when confronted with ideas involving these. Very often, people follow the lead of a boss or a strong personality. He rejects, they reject. He accepts, they accept. Also, in addition to the blurring we mentioned in Chapter 9, it's sometimes difficult to distinguish between a negative orientation and a rejection of a new idea based on its palpable impracticality.

The point is that, while in most cases Exhibit 14 can be used to spot, often in seconds, an individual's or group's orientation, in other cases patterns must be ferreted out, going through a process of "response filtration" to sort out these areas of impreciseness. "Response filtration" may sound imposing (which is why I threw it in), but actually once the principle in Exhibit 14 is absorbed (which ought to take all of two or three minutes) and is used for a bit in assessing orientations when new ideas are introduced, I've found that a surprisingly high percentage of people exposed to it do develop the ability to sense the two orientations without much conscious effort. Toss in a little conscious effort, and the ability to determine *why* people are oriented the way they are (causes of negative orientation, Chapter 9) can also fall into place. This not only helps people read an individual's or group's orientation and understand the organization better but additionally becomes extremely useful in dealing with the individual or group on a practical basis.

Another method to identify new-idea orientation is simply to ask the people who ought to know (but may not know they know until forced to think about it) to fill out a questionnaire.

TECHNIQUE

The technique is different from the one we used in identifying tempo. When I first developed the following questionnaire, I attempted to use the same procedure (small groups, cross-table discussions, and so on). Two tries. Two bombs. It didn't work because, unlike discussions of tempo, which most could view with some objectivity, group discussions of new-idea orientation tended to degenerate into polarized rehashes of the merits of the ideas themselves. What did work was submitting the questionnaire to every executive (not just a cross-section), with instructions to return it within a week. (The timing is important. If less than a week is allowed, the answers tend to be rushed and vague. If more than a week is allowed, the questionnaire tends to get put off until the last minute, with equally poor results.) One important point: Anybody within the organization who has contact with the outside world, especially salesmen, should be included.

The questionnaire format consists of five parts:

1. An introduction explaining that the purpose is to help the organization become more receptive to new ideas, emphasizing that the only way the company is going to grow (or grow faster) or make money (or make more money) is by becoming more responsive to new ideas. ("Techniques change,

attitudes change, business climates change, technology changes, people's habits change, product needs change. Change is a continuous process. If the response to these changes becomes static, then we're heading for trouble. But if by becoming more alert to new ideas, we can anticipate and move with the change, they can be turned to our advantage.")

2. A short piece on orientations and how they impact on new ideas. The contrasts between "risk" and "opportunity" overviews is not only graphic but easily related to.

3. A review of Exhibit 14 with the explanation, which can be lifted in toto from Chapter 9.

4. A firm statement not only identifying the persons (or person) who will review the questionnaire but giving assurance that all replies will remain confidential.

5. And finally, the questions that appear on the following pages:

QUESTIONNAIRE_____

Section 1

Select one or two of our competitors and as specifically as possible indicate one or two areas where you think either one is doing a better job than we are. The following are some of the areas you might consider, but don't feel limited to these:

Product line
Product quality
Product pricing
Product R&D
Selling effort
Support of salesmen's efforts
Marketing (distribution channels, sales promotions, and so on)

Manufacturing (processes, procedures, equipment, costs, and
   so on)
Labor relations
General level of aggressiveness (with an example)
Reaction time to problems and opportunities (with examples)
Purchasing policies
Plant or product diversification
Customer service (field and other)
Corporate image

(a) In the categories you selected, briefly explain in what way
you think the competitors are doing a better job. Note for each
how long you think it's been doing a better job. (Check one:
Weeks   Months   Years)

(b) In the categories you selected, did we ever try to follow
their lead? Did we perhaps even start out ahead of them? In either
case, are they ahead of us now because we failed to make or
sustain a full-scale commitment? Did they take a basic idea we
both had and implement it faster or better? If we were ahead at
one time, what do you think we did or didn't do that let our
advantage slip away? Explain.

(c) If we have not tried to follow their lead, do you think we
should have? Have we ever considered doing so, and if so, what
happened to our good intentions? Did we fall victim to inertia,
indifference, a failure to coordinate our efforts? Did management
fail somewhere along the line to support or inspire the effort?
Did we perhaps try a different approach rather than simply follow
their lead? If so, what happened?

(d) Or did we simply conclude that it was "not such a good
idea in light of our particular situation at that particular time" to
follow their lead? If so, what was our rationale for this conclusion? Does it appear in retrospect that that rationale represented
a valid judgment? Was there at that time a clear-cut division of
opinion within the organization, or did we simply agree by not
disagreeing? Did we ever rationalize our failure to act on the

basis that to do so was simply too expensive? If so, do you think in retrospect that was a valid argument?

(e) Are we taking effective steps now to narrow the gaps or to move ahead? If not, or if the steps we're taking are half-hearted, what's holding us back? Explain. Is there an unresolved division of opinion on what steps to take?

Section 2

Among other things, the new-idea creative process is generally inhibited by one or more of the following:

- Personal timidity: fear of making a commitment to a new idea because of the risk of failure or the fear of having to actively implement a new idea and take responsibility for this implementation.
- Inability or unwillingness to recognize possible potential benefits of new ideas.
- Lack of individual competence to deal with and control problems of implementation.
- Organizational lethargy or reluctance to move off ground zero into new unfamiliar ground.
- Individual reluctance to endorse new ideas because it may result in additional job responsibilities.
- Lack of support for new ideas because they are "someone else's."
- Lack of well-defined and well-communicated company goals and objectives into which new ideas can be tied.
- Leadership that's remote from areas of potential impact of new ideas.
- Poor organizational tempo, creating a potentially frustrating milieu for implementing new ideas.
- Long time lapses between ideas, decisions, and decision implementation, taking the "enthusiasm edge" off new-idea development.

- Lack of tolerance for honest, nonrepetitive mistakes as a learning process.
- Lack of real or sufficient delegation, discouraging the development of the individual problem-solving skills needed to encourage and aggressively implement new ideas.
- Organizational attitude or policies discouraging a spirit of individual "entrepreneurship."
- A cumbersome approval process, requiring so many approval points that enthusiasm for introducing new ideas is squelched.
- An organizational attitude that places primary thrust on the *risk* aspects of new ideas as opposed to their *opportunity* aspects.

Now take the areas you listed in which our competition is doing a better job. Run down the above list and put a check opposite any item you think may be responsible for our being behind in the first area you listed in Section 1. If you named a second area, repeat the process, using a circle instead of a check.

Section 3

List what you consider to be one or two of our current major problems or general problem areas.

(a) To the best of your knowledge, are we presently doing something about them? If we are, are we doing it in little steps rather than trying to clobber them in one or two fell swoops? How successful have our efforts been?

(b) If the problem or problem area is of recent vintage and we're not now actually taking remedial steps, are we at least seriously discussing doing something about it? If so, how long have we been "discussing" this? If the answer is months or longer, is it a question of our knowing what to do but simply not getting it done? If so, any idea what is holding us back?

(c) Have we reached the alternative-weighing stage yet? Have remedial ideas been presented and either rejected or not acted on? Purely as a subjective judgment, do you think some of the rejected ideas have merit? If so, go back to the list of new-idea creative process inhibitors (Section 2) and put an "x" opposite those items you think might account for the rejection or the failure to act.

Section 4

Now let's shift gears and look on the bright side. List one or two areas where you think we're doing a better job than our competition or our industry as a whole. Or, if we're not ahead, where are we at least one of the leaders? Whatever we did in those areas to achieve this position, did we originate or refine the ideas or techniques or did they originate somewhere else and are we ahead because we're doing a better job of implementing them?

Section 5

Let's get some of your impressions.

(a) Do you think the people you work with or others within our organization with whom you come in contact are generally thinking creatively about our problems and opportunities and expressing their ideas freely, or do you get the feeling that for some reason, perhaps because of previous frustrations in getting someone to listen seriously, they're holding back? If the latter, is this (circle one) widespread, mixed, or not a major problem?

(b) Would you say we're a "good listening" (receptive) organization? How would you rate (good, fair, bad) each of the following in the "good listening" department: top management, upper-middle, middle, lower?

(c) Are we, in your opinion, too rigidly organized and too tightly crammed into our job routines to encourage a free flow of ideas? Are we a "do your own job and mind your own business" organization, or are we loose enough to invite and encourage a good cross-current of new ideas and suggestions? If the former, is this creating any tensions in our working environment?

(d) To put it another way, would you say we are a creative organization? Do we have creative people who have a pretty receptive audience for their ideas? Or do we have creative people lacking a responsive forum for their ideas? Or do we lack creative people whose imaginations can provide signposts to future success?

(e) Taking your answers to the previous sections into consideration, would you say our present trend is toward becoming an overall pacesetter in our industry, a close-behind follower of the leaders, a way-behind follower, or somewhere in the middle?

(f) Now suppose you were suddenly appointed General Manager of New ideas with the job (and authority) of making us more responsive to new ideas, how would you organize the effort or what kind of a program would you set up? State first, if you will, any organizational problems you think you'd have to overcome, and then indicate how you would deal with them.

BASIS FOR ANALYSIS

Section 1 is aimed at establishing the negative side of the comparison with other companies (Is your company a follower or a laggard?). Section 2 is designed to pinpoint some of the causes of this negative position, while Section 3 is designed to confirm from a different direction the conclusions reached by the responses to Section 1. The purpose of Section 4 is to give the comparison some balance and identify some of the organization's positively oriented areas as well as pick up any significant differences of opinion.

Essentially, the first three sections are designed to determine in what areas the organization is negatively oriented by assessing its negative responsiveness to change. In the absence of any means to quantify this, the best gauge is to tie that responsiveness to where the organization stands in relation to its competition, on the premise that both the organization and its competition are chasing the same dollar in the same marketplace and are facing essentially the same problems and opportunities.

These first three sections do, of course, interrelate. For example, if a consensus of answers to Section 1 suggests that the product line lags behind the competition's and a consensus out of Section 3 confirms that a primary problem area is the product line and failure to update it, then it's a pretty good clue that somewhere the people responsible for the product line are negatively oriented (or incompetent) and are not responding to changing needs. It could be the people directly responsible, or it could be that higher levels of management are restraining them. All three sections can contribute to identifying both the who and the why.

Section 5, stressing how the organization perceives itself, is designed to confirm the responses to the first four sections. On paper an organization can have the most enlightened structure and the most sophisticated operating procedures in 16 states and Baltimore, but if it doesn't perceive itself as aggressive and hungry for and receptive to new ideas, you can damn well bet it won't be. These perceptions are one of the critical keys in the process of analysis, since perceptions tend to be not only revealing but self-fulfilling.

CAVEATS

There are, of course, some caveats to be considered in the analysis. A company can correctly perceive itself as being highly receptive to new ideas and thus consider itself positively oriented. However, receptivity itself is no guarantee of success. The company can still fail because the ideas to which it is receptive may be terrible, poorly implemented, or untimely. Incompetence, therefore, not positive receptivity becomes the problem in this case.

Often some executives are simply not in a position to accurately know what the competition is up to, and some of the replies may have a goodly dose of blue-sky, wishful thinking or reflect internal sour grapes. The questionnaire opens the door for expressing some highly subjective and self-serving opinions and for venting frustration. These should be, where possible, identified for what they are and filtered out in the analysis procedure.

In some cases it may be that the organization's attitudes are so inbred and work habits so tightly patterned that it is incapable of developing enough perspective to make the questionnaire effective. (I haven't run across this yet, but it is a possibility that should be mentioned.)

If the stage is properly set by the person administering the questionnaire, more perspective and frankness should come out of it than self-serving finger pointing, and the process of analysis can be as cut-and-dried as it is revealing. In some cases, however, the problem source can be somewhat remote from the problem area and thus be less obvious to the naked eye. It is in these areas that the value of the questionnaire takes on added significance. The following two cases illustrate this point.

CASE 1

XYZ Corporation. Northeast. Corrugated carton manufacturer. Four plants. Sales approximately $125 million. Founder-family owned. President, major stockholder, midsixties, shrewd, paternalistic. Executive VP, younger brother, midfifties, lesser stockholder, more authoritarian, less agreeable. Questionnaire given to 104 people, including 41 salesmen. Assurance given that only the president and one outsider would see the replies.

Questionnaire Responses

Section 1: Among the production staffs (executives and engineers, especially at lower levels), a high percentage agreed that top competitors were ahead in production technology. This somewhat solid bloc contrasted sharply with the rest of the respondents, whose answers were scattered rather thinly across categories.

Section 2: Personal timidity, lack of well-defined company goals, leadership remote from areas of potential impact of new ideas, lack of tolerance for honest nonrepetitive mistakes as a learning process, lack of real and sufficient delegation, discouragement of an entrepreneurial spirit (17 out of 28 lower-level production executives and engineers named this last factor) all scored high by the production people as causes of the company's lack of leadership in the area of production technology.

Section 3: As expected, the lower echelons of production people named production technology as a primary problem area and pretty much rechecked the same items as on the Section 2 list. Strangely, no other segment of the organization (except for a few scattered individuals) zeroed in on production technology as a problem area.

Section 4: In fact, almost the entire sales force listed production technology as a strength, as did most others. This enthusiasm was obviously not shared by their production colleagues.

Section 5: The answers to this final section continued the division. Most everybody seemed content with the organization's ability to encourage and listen to new ideas except, as would be expected, the production groups. They indicated that the company was "too rigidly organized" to encourage a free flow of ideas, and top management took its lumps as not being a "good listening" segment of the organization. Nineteen out of the 28 production people thought that the organization had good creative people who weren't being listened to. Their answers to the rest of Section 5 sustained their negative impression. In the last part, asking what they would do if they were appointed general manager of new ideas, 22 out of 28 suggested the company dump its management by objectives program.

A Confusing Picture

The questionnaire responses obviously presented a head-scratching dichotomy. The majority of nonproduction executives expressed the opinion that the company's production technology was a basic strength and point of industry leadership and that the organization itself was essentially positively oriented. But the production staffs, responsible in large measure for this leadership, felt just the opposite.

If this reaction had been confined to one plant, a hard look at that plant's management would probably have turned up a source of negative orientation. But all four plants were involved. Further, the company was well capitalized, and top management had never shown any qualms about spending money for capital improvements. The VP of manufacturing—diligent, knowledgeable, and likable—delegated a lot of authority to his plant managers, who for the most part assumed it with competence. Significantly, however, his questionnaire answers were at almost total variance from his production people's. In Section 1, he did not indict production technology as being behind the competition's. In Section 3, he stated that production technology was a current problem only because of

constant changes taking place in the industry and that consequently a continuing major effort was, is, and always would
be under way to improve technology. In Section 4, he listed
production technology as one of the company's strong points
in terms of industry leadership.

His reaction only added to the apparently confusing results.
If there was a problem, it didn't seem likely on the surface that
he was contributing to it, nor was there any apparent negative
contribution by top management, which had a history of being
willing to support most requests for technological improvements. Yet blocs of production people at all four plants felt the
organization was not geared to positive responses to the needs
of the production department.

The Plot Thickens

Once the location of the organization's *apparent* negative orientation had been pinpointed, the next step was to determine
the source, and the key to this lay in the gratuitous suggestion
by 22 production people that the company dump its MBO program. Tracing back from there, it appeared that the villain of
the piece was Younger Brother Executive VP. Older Brother
President was courtly, benign, paternalistic, with a quiet inner
toughness, and he seldom raised his voice. ("Make an old man
happy and do it for me," he would say softly to any executive
who argued against carrying out a presidential directive, and
few wanted to chance making the old man unhappy, especially
since he was generally right.) When the president suffered a
mild stroke, Younger Brother Executive VP became the effective chief executive and operating officer.

Enter on the scene at this time a consultant who promptly
convinced the executive VP that he'd better start an MBO program before the company plunged into the abyss. (What abyss
was never quite explained; the company was, up till this time,

making more money than ever.) The executive VP, impatient, curt, often intimidating, and a business school graduate who had always felt that Older Brother had run the company with the same unenlightened, unstructured principles that scored big in the late nineteenth century, waded in. He decided to introduce the MBO program with the production groups with the eventual purpose of extending it throughout the company.

The consultant obligingly prepared a master program, bound in two loose-leaf notebooks totaling 84 pages (16 of which dealt with a brief history of MBO. Oh boy!). The emphasis was heavy, as would be expected, on tying achievement of objectives to pay raises, promotions, and the like. The program was to be funneled through the VP of manufacturing, thence to the plant managers, and from them to the subordinate levels. Regarding this as a turnaround situation (from what to what was never made quite clear) and wanting to prove a point and have an effective program in place as a fait accompli before Older Brother came back, the executive VP made it pretty clear at plant meetings that each production staff member had to not only come up with a healthy number of objectives but then hit pretty close to 100 percent achievement or his future with the company was going to be pretty grim. This was a new ball game, kids.

The plant managers were told that if their staff people didn't achieve close to 100 percent of their objectives it would reflect adversely on the manager's ability to lead and guide, so they tended to approve those objectives that were easiest to achieve. Similarly, the VP of manufacturing was told that if his plant managers didn't come through it would be considered that he didn't either. The VP of manufacturing, no dummy and no hero, took cover. "The program was going to work, dammit, or else," said the executive VP.

He was savage in playing the numbers game, and this turned out to be the kicker. The plant people selected unimportant, little objectives blown up in their descriptions to sound like great leaps forward, a ploy that eluded the marketing-oriented executive VP. While many in number (many had in fact already been started and were well on the road to completion), they were small in scope, involving precious little risk of not being achievable. Most of the troops hit their first six-months' targets 100 percent. (These were the "little steps" that about 80 percent responded affirmatively to in Section 3. This admission served to confirm that the production staffs had responded to the questionnaire without fear or restraint, a fact that probably would not have been the case had they not been assured that Older Brother President would be the only person within the company to see their responses.)

The Plot Unthickens

Seven months after the introduction of the MBO program, Older Brother, fully recovered, came back on the scene. He was impressed with the apparent results of the program. But after a few plant visits, he sensed a certain uptightness among the production staffs and plant managers with whom he had always had a warm, open, give-and-take relationship. When he mentioned this to Younger Brother Executive VP, the latter assured him that the MBO program in terms of number of objectives and achievement rate spoke for itself and he suggested that perhaps the uptightness was due to the fact that the production staffs finally had to go to work and have their efforts individually measured. Sounded reasonable. But still Older Brother wasn't too sure. Ergo, at his direction, the questionnaire.

The Light at the End of the Tunnel

Going in, the MBO program had two strikes against it. First, given the company's paternalistic, informal type of management structure, the close cooperation among the various production people, their general competence levels, and their success in doing what they were supposed to do, there was no compelling reason for an MBO program. It could, and apparently did, under these conditions serve only to throw the old successful modus operandi off balance. Second, the program was force fed with little chance for discussion or for any justifiable accommodation to the previous way of operating. This hardly inspired cooperation. While they were dragooned into following the letter of the program, the production staffs quickly deep-sixed the spirit.

The questionnaire had pinpointed a newborn pocket of negative orientation along with its cause, fortunately before its impact could be significantly felt on the manufacturing process. This negative orientation took the form of not only discouraging the expression of new ideas and the willingness to accept them (since they would have been added to the already long lists of objectives) but also the reluctance to advance any new programs that involved a great degree of risk because these could jeopardize achievement rates.

Thus, we could reasonably speculate that, if unchecked, the cumulative effects of the MBO program—especially in terms of masking the big problems and opportunities as they came along because of the built-in reluctance to consider the big solutions (read "high-risk solutions") such problems and opportunities would have called for—would have over a period of time resulted in a slippage of the company's production technology leadership. For example, the staff at one plant had been working on a new wax-coating process when the program was instituted. If past experience with such projects was any guide, it was a pretty good bet that they would have come up with a breakthrough technique. However, because of the amount of development costs necessary to finally prove it—a high-risk venture with a high benefit potential—and the question of who in this team effort would get saddled with the "objective," the project was very neatly and unobstrusively put into limbo.

Footnote

Since production technology was still in great shape, the questionnaire responses were obviously exaggerated to prove a point—in this case, a very valid point. It would have been naive not to suspect that there had been considerable communication, if not outright collusion, between the various plant staffs during the week of questionnaire response preparation, which in this case was fine because it resulted in some highly cohesive blocs of responses that simplified the analysis.

When the dust cleared, the MBO program was booted out. The president is back to patting heads and exhorting his people "to make an old man happy," the production staffs are back to work doing what they do best (three weeks after the demise of the program, the new wax-coating process came into being), and the executive VP is back to concentrating on what he does best, the marketing effort. But he's still heard muttering from time to time.

CASE 2

ABC Industries. Stereo speaker and turntable manufacturer. Northeast. Sales: approximately $57 million. Two buildings, same industrial park: one manufacturing, one R&D and administrative. People questioned, 54 including engineers and 17 salesmen. Special note: Reason for questionnaire—selling prices reflecting manufacturing costs were pricing the company out of its market. Top management couldn't seem to get a fix on the cause.

Questionnaire Responses

Section 1: Twenty-eight respondents suggested that the company lagged behind the competition in manufacturing. One significant note: In the past year, the company had hired one new buyer (out of four in the department), one assistant production manager, and one senior manufacturing engineer, all of whom had been hired away from competitors. All three, with some perspective on "how it was done elsewhere," enthusiastically joined this "we're behind the competition in manufacturing" parade. Attesting to the cost effect of these manufacturing difficulties, 13 out of 17 salesmen noted that the competition was beginning to clobber them pricewise in the marketplace; 14 out of 17 also noted that lack of on-time deliveries gave the company another disadvantage vis-à-vis its competition. So far, no surprises.

Six out of eight R&D engineers (here again, as with the preceding case, collusion in response preparation was pretty obvious) felt that the company's purchasing policies were out of sync with the department's needs and thus were another area in which the company lagged behind. They were joined by the new buyer and the new senior manufacturing engineer as well as seven production engineers and executives.

Section 2: "Inability to recognize the potential of new ideas" rang in a fairly high score among both production and R&D staffs, as did "long time lapses between ideas, decisions, and decision implementation." "An organizational attitude discouraging a spirit of individual 'entrepreneurship' " and "an organizational attitude that places primary thrust on risk aspects of new ideas as opposed to opportunity aspects" led the R&D parade.

Section 3 generally confirmed the responses to Sections 1 and 2, as the categories selected in Section 1 were picked also as present major problem areas. Section 4 confirmed it through the back door, since only people generally remote from manufacturing and its problems listed manufacturing as a leadership segment.

Section 5 coupled with explanatory responses to the previous questions nailed down the source of the problem.

What Happened

A quick review of the questionnaire results left little doubt that the manufacturing department was not operating smoothly and that R&D was operating in a *non*-self-imposed strait-jacket. The *source* of the problem lay with neither one. Both the questionnaire and postquestionnaire investigation narrowed the source to one person—the director of purchasing.

A long-time executive of the company (one of those, present in virtually every company, who could recall wistfully how "things were in the old days"), he was able to exercise his authority and extend influence well beyond this title.

His long tenure and strong personality gave him clout with the very top levels of management.

Several years before, the company's equally long-time production manager had served as his own materials manager. He left the company, and a new production manager was hired from outside. Because the new manager was unfamiliar with materials sources, the specifics of materials scheduling, and inventory requirements, the director of purchasing took over this function while the new production manager "learned the ropes." But he never let go and after a short period of time, no one in top management questioned his dual role as materials manager and director of purchasing. This did, however, give him considerable influence over the manufacturing department—so much so that, when two successive production managers rebelled at this influence, he was able to use his clout with top management to banana-peel both out the door marked "You don't work here anymore."

For a while, this presented no serious problem, aside from disgruntled production managers. Manufacturing materials flowed in as needed, and the R&D department functioned effectively. Then came two events. First, it was discovered that a cabinet supplier had been tucking it to the company. As a long-time supplier, prompt deliverer, overall reliable source of quality cabinets, it occupied a unique position. Not only was it the sole cabinet supplier, but the door was closed to any other cabinet supplier asking for a shot at the business. It was not bashful in taking advantage of this position. Its prices edged up until they were 20–25 percent higher than the market justified.

During the same time that this came to light, the industry was plunged into a recession. The company lost money, and a frantic campaign was introduced to cut costs. The director of purchasing felt that both the recession and the cabinet supplier's shenanigans were personal affronts to him. So he picked up his sledgehammer and went to work. Determined not to get nailed again, he required all his buyers to solicit at least four quotes on every purchase they made and "never mind this business of justifying a higher price because a supplier is 'reliable.' The world is full of 'reliable' suppliers." The new vendor-selection criterion was price. Low man gets the order, period. No exceptions.

So far as manufacturing was concerned, two things happened, and neither was good. Requisitions for materials funneled through the materials manager–director of purchasing. From him, they went to the buyer assigned to order the materials. He had to get his four quotes. This took time. Then the purchase order itself had to be countersigned by the director of purchasing, who first reviewed the four quotes. This took time. Meanwhile, the plant frequently ran out of whatever it needed, and the gears often sputtered to a halt. This running in fits and starts had an obvious effect on costs as well as on the company's ability to make timely deliveries. Further, when orders were placed with vendors, they were not always the same vendors who supplied the previous orders. Mix-ups occurred; quality rejects abounded. More delays.

Vendors who knew the company, who had built a relationship with it, who understood its requirements and how to service those requirements were suddenly frozen out by low-ball-ers who either wanted desperately to get started with the company or just plain needed the business and who managed cost reductions by fiddling with quality. Recognizing that "loyalty" was no longer a part of the company's purchase decision, most of the old suppliers shut off whatever help and industry intelligence they used to provide the company as a matter of course. The company was, of course, buying at rock-bottom prices (a fact the director of purchasing made sure top management was made constantly aware of and for which he was just as constantly applauded). In time, ragged service and quality of purchased materials was accepted as a fact of life that just had to be endured. ("It isn't like the old days," the director of purchasing would sigh, "when people took pride in what they did.")

R&D, which up to the point of change in purchasing philosophy had for the most part dealt directly with suppliers on new product development and relied to a large extent on their design and materials input, now lost this help. They could no longer promise the first order to those vendors who contributed to this effort. Everything now, even at this stage, had to go through purchasing. "The purchasing department's function is to buy," the director told R&D. "We can't control a damn thing if you people go off on your own." (This reached a new height of absurdity when a development engineer wanted to try a new type of latex glue for a unit he was redesigning. Following procedure, a buyer had to go out for four quotes at an estimated cost of $11 per request and four weeks in time. In the meantime, the frustrated engineer went around the corner to his favorite ye olde hardware shoppe and on his own bought a tube for $1.13).

So the negative orientation in this case was manifested primarily through the purchasing director's emphasis on risk rather than *opportunity*. For example, if someone in manufacturing wanted to develop a new procedure and it required a purchase of anything, it had to go, of course, through the director. "You know how much it costs? Why do you need it?" he would snarl (not "What will it do for us?"). All this frayed nerves, ate up time, and tended to dull any enthusiasm the new idea might have generated.

Case in point: A senior manufacturing engineer wanted to extend a conveyor line to bridge an area that now involved hand carrying. The new conveyors and controls amounted to a one-shot cost of approximately $11,000. Savings on the two people it would replace was approximately $23,000 per year. The production manager signed off on the project. "Let's do it," he told the engineer. The latter went to the director of purchasing. "$11,000 is a lot of money," he was told. "What if it doesn't work?" "It'll work." "Show me." The process of trying to convince the director of purchasing took about two weeks, off and on. Finally, the director relented. "We'll shop around." The conveyor system finally came in—seven weeks later. "We got it cheaper," said the director pointedly, "only $7,200." "Great," said the engineer. "Only it won't work. It's not the kind I asked for." The engineer went to the production manager. "To hell with it," the engineer said. "It's futile. I'm quitting." He did.

Further, new ideas had to be generated in vacuums, with little if any effective outside help or encouragement. This too took a whole lot of edge off any enthusiasm for coming up with new ideas.

The Tag Line

Before the questionnaire, top management had not been fully aware of what had been happening. Until then, it considered the diligence of the director of purchasing in watching company dollars like a two-headed, four-eyed hawk as not only commendable but the product of a highly effective and dedicated purchasing organization. Management was comforted by his input of long hours (10–11 a day), which it viewed as more evidence of his diligence, thoroughness, and dedication. It had accepted the problem of spot materials shortages ("We can't order far ahead because we can't predict which style of speakers we'll get a run on") as inherent in the way businesses such as theirs had to operate with today's "high cost of inventories."

But what they had regarded as an organizational oasis of cost control in a desert of seemingly unbridled rising costs turned out, when stripped naked by the questionnaire, to be one executive in a key middle-management spot fouling up the gears of the manufacturing process, hobbling the efforts of the R&D department, and successfully drying up the creative juices of these two key departments because of his negative orientation (mixed perhaps with some reluctance to encourage other people's ideas because they might produce a rising star in opposition to his own).

After two weeks of fighting a savage rearguard action, the director of purchasing was persuaded to "retire"—a fact, sad to say, few people in the organization had cause to seriously lament. The new director of purchasing concentrated on redeveloping effective relationships with suppliers, and manufacturing was given back control of materials management. The plant shortly thereafter resumed its "hum." Costs dropped about 8 percent in the first seven months because of adequate materials inventories, less downtime, more responsive scheduling, and faster development of new plant efficiency techniques. R&D responded to the freer hand, and sales responded to the stabilized pricing, better quality, and on-time delivery.

The organizational climate now produced the attitude that new ideas were potential opportunities rather than probable risks. Positive orientation struck again!

CHAPTER 11

Listening—The Superhighway to Positive Orientation

A true story:

A medium-size division of a giant electronics company, housed in an old converted mill building in a rural section of the Midwest, had (unlike the rest of the company's divisions) no union. Morale was fair.

The plant manager—staid, conservative, with a reputation for fairness, if not outstanding competence—retired after 16 years. He was replaced by an aggressive up-and-comer, who shortly after coming aboard began step by step to renovate the manufacturing spaces, painting here, glassing-in walls there. When he heard that his production people were disturbed because their toilet facilities were drab, dirty, with old fixtures that were being invidiously compared to the modern, squeaky clean executive washrooms, he had the workers' washrooms torn out and replaced with replicas of the executive washrooms. (During this same period, a chronic production line bottleneck was broken by speeding up the line from 12 seconds per unit to 10 seconds. No one complained. You can see why this guy was considered an up-and-comer.)

However, a short eight months after his arrival, he was promoted to divisional general manager and transferred. Back at the ranch, the plant went into a mild state of depression. Morale plummeted. Were they once again going to be consigned to the backwaters of the company? "Not so," said their group

VP at headquarters, who was soon on a plane to the plant. Breaking the executive staff into groups, he assured each that whoever the (as yet unnamed) replacement was to be he would carry on the work of the previous manager. Scotching a persistent rumor, no, the plant was not going to be phased out.

Satisfied, he left. Then reports began to filter back. The banner of rejection still hung limply from the plant's jackstaff. "What more can I do?" asked the VP. "Simple," he was told. "Get back on the plane and talk to the *workers* on the production line." A notice went up that the VP would be making a plant tour on such-and-such a date (two days) and was looking forward to chatting with everyone.

He toured the plant, in shirt-sleeves, tie askew, asking questions, showing interest, intimating that the plant was a jewel in the crown of the empire, noting what a great job the former plant manager did and how the new one, when named, would do the same. But more than anything, he *listened*—and *they* listened. In fact, together, they listened the depression away. (Sit on the word *listen* for a bit. You'll see how cleverly we come back to it to develop a point.)

During the 1970s and 1980s, after the frenzy of MBO had spent itself in over 700 books and articles and a zillion seminars, a favorite pastime among business writers, lecturers, consultants looking for a cause, seminar sponsors, business school academics, and the like has been to take up the cudgels for duplicating the Japanese experience. The exhortation is that we'd better do something pretty quick before they ace us out of every market in sight. Unhappily, the argument has considerable merit.

The Japanese, of course, operate in a climate uniquely suited to their experience: their ethnic homogeneity and homogeneous work ethic; the absence of an inherent adversarial labor–

management climate; their loyalty toward authority, evolving through the centuries from the clan to the warlord to the emperor and finally to economic authority (that is, the paternalistic employer organization with its reciprocal loyalty); their recognition that their lack of natural resources means that survival depends on exporting in order to import and that exporting depends largely on making better products. Despite these differences in background, culture, and circumstances between them and us, the fact remains they do have a lot to teach us. But there is no great mystique to what that is.

Very simply, most of the Japanese industries we compete against are oriented on the *far end* of the positive spectrum, and the key to the development of this positive orientation lies in the word *listen*. (See? Told you we'd work it back in.) They listen. When someone listens, someone else becomes involved, and this involvement is the essence of participation. Listening, wanting to listen, and providing the opportunity for someone to be listened to is the culture medium in which participation grows. And effective participation, in the broad sense, attested to by the Japanese experience, is what builds the foundation for a two-way loyalty. Listening, unfortunately, is a lost art in America. We hear sounds, we hear words, we hear "intrusions," but we don't listen. And when we don't listen, we set up frustrations, distrusts, adversaries, or people who just don't care—not participants.

A FACT OF BUSINESS LIFE

Every organization is continually challenged by problems and opportunities, and there's just no way a problem can be solved or an opportunity taken advantage of until it is identified and assessed and a course of action decided on and then implemented. That's the "what." New ideas and new apprroaches are the "how." (That's logical. If the old still worked, chances are there wouldn't be a problem, huh?) If an organization is not receptive to new ideas, if those ideas do not fall on imaginative, creative, responsive, discriminating, aggressive ears, if the ground on which they fall is not preplowed and made fertile for their growth, then, as the man says, "There ain't no 'how' and that ends the 'what.'" Success, often survival itself, and negative orientation are a contradiction in terms.

Because the inherent inclination toward negativism is always there as a course of least resistance and seemingly least risk, if an organization is indifferent toward its orientation, this negativism just naturally falls into place. Thus, it takes activity (doing *some*thing) in contrast to passivity (doing *no*thing) to overcome this natural tilt. But once an organization has taken the proper steps to create a positively oriented environment, as have many Japanese business institutions, and once it has tasted enough success to develop some level of confidence, the tendency is for that positive orientation to sustain itself. But let up on the pressure or backtrack on some of the elements that contribute to this environment (like stopping listening), and backsliding is inevitable. This then is a call for action! (Drum roll, trumpet fanfare, unfurled flag, moist eyes.)

PUTTING LISTENING TO WORK

The following case is actually a composite of two organizations. It will, perhaps, sum up the principle of positive orientation and the taking of positive action with its dependence on listening. We will trace the origins of this action, its development, and what finally happened. It was not a smooth path, and we'll include the false starts and pitfalls because they represent insidious traps that can be avoided if we're alert to the fact that they lurk along the way.

The Program Gets Started

The president of a rubber processing company, just beginning to feel the pinch of Japanese competition, attended a seminar on Japanese Circles of Quality, participative management techniques, and various other things. Impressed, he decided he'd better get aboard the bandwagon, like forthwith. With more enthusiasm than understanding, he made the board-room, with its plush chairs, soft lighting, and imposing inlaid rectangular table, available to the various circles he set up. Each circle, 12 altogether, consisted of seven or eight production employee representatives and one junior executive or engi-neer. Each circle met once a month at staggered times. The theme was, he felt, a stirring call to arms: "Tell us what's on your minds, no holds barred. Tell us how we can make a bet-ter product and make it less costly."

The executive heading each circle, representing manage-ment, was assigned to chair the meeting and to submit a brief summary of each meeting to his department head. Great move, thought the president. This is truly enlightened management. The troops will love it, this opportunity and encouragement to express themselves creatively. We'll beat the Japanese at their own game and out-circle their circles.

They did. The result was one big circle, a zero. The prob-lem? Several. First of all, the circle was not a circle. It was an inlaid walnut rectangular table. (More about this later.) The chairing executive didn't join the circle, he presided over it.⁵ Because he was a junior executive, he had little authority to effectively take action on any suggestion, because this was up to his department head. ("Let 'em blow off steam," the general manager of operations told them. "But don't let them mouse-trap you. Listen, but don't, whatever you do, make any com-mitments you may have to backtrack on.")

Sensing that they would invite trouble if they encouraged

too many ideas they thought their department heads wouldn't support (which was virtually every one), the chairing executives tried to stifle many of the ideas on the spot. ("You just don't understand how it works," was their favorite, and maddening, put-down.) They didn't cherish the idea of becoming banner carriers for the production line workers and thus becoming too closely identified with them. Bad politics, they reasoned. So they didn't really listen. They certainly didn't listen to new ideas as possible opportunities. They only heard words that could be a threat to their otherwise comfortable corporate and career well-being.

In a self-fulfilling prophecy, higher executives, who had gone into the program with little enthusiasm in the first place, felt the meetings were unproductive and a waste of time. Their indifference (if not contempt) was soon sensed below. They felt no pressure to make the program work, because the president, confident that setting up a functional structure was enough and that everyone would respond to it as enthusiastically as he did, paid only minimal attention to the program once it was in place. It quickly fell apart. The circles degenerated into grievance committees, and inevitably the stronger, more vocal, more militant employees took over, while the others sat passively by wondering what the hell they were doing there. Fewer and fewer ideas were proposed, and the participants began to skip meetings in droves. ("My kid has a little league game." In February!!? "I have a stiff neck." "My wife's cousin Marylou Beth was gored by a rhinocerous.") The president sought help, and the program was revamped.

Developing the Program

The first step was for the president to spend a day wandering through the plant stressing a new tone for the meetings. The circles were not to be grievance committees, he explained, although suggestions for making working conditions less boring and more pleasant would, of course, be welcome. The purpose of the circles was to create a means for mutual cooperation, to help create a company that would show the world that this was the best damn company, with the best damn product, made by the smartest damn people in the world. He needed their help and besides, he noted, the best guarantee for everybody's job security and advancement was to stave off the enemy by making the best product at the lowest possible cost.

The second step was to transform a corner of the plant into a "circle conference room." No longer did they have to meet in the intimidating and patronizing atmosphere of the boardroom as "guests" of the company. The room, light and airy, was equipped with comfortable armchairs (not plush), a coffee machine (with doughnuts and Danish supplied by the company), and a *round table*.

Seemingly a nit-picking minor point, the round table was in fact quite significant. All other conditions being equal, the shape of the table can and generally does set the tone for either consensus or conflict—and round lends itself to consensus, whereas square or rectangular lends itself to polarization and conflict.

At the same time, the president laid down the objectives to the management team. "This is not a gimmick program," he told them, "not a clever device to defuse any pent-up labor–management tensions but rather a way to take all the brain power and experience in the organization and concentrate it on product and cost improvement. I'm providing the structure You make it work. You can bet that this time I'll be monitoring it every step of the way."

The third step was to convene the circles not with one executive (white-collared engineers were included in the executive group) but with two—one as before from the same department as the production employees, and, for greater objectivity and wider involvement, one from somewhere outside the department. Told not to sit together, they no longer held the exclusive right to the chairmanship of the meetings. It rotated with each meeting so that the majority of meetings were chaired by one of the production employees. Every idea, beef, or suggestion was noted by the outside executive. At the end of each meeting, he read his notes to the group, a brief précis of the ideas or complaints brought up, and a very brief summary of the arguments for and against. The group had to assent that each was a fair representation of what had been discussed.

Between meetings, the two executives and the meeting's chairman (or a production employee representative, if one of the two executives had chaired the meeting) met as a committee, then reviewed the notes with the appropriate department head. At the next circle meeting, this committee reported on the steps that would or would not be taken on the suggestions made at the previous meeting. For those that would be taken, an implementation schedule was agreed upon. For those that would not be taken or required more development, the reasons were carefully explained.

One happy circumstance began to emerge, though not yet in full bloom. Whereas before, the production employees had addressed their remarks to a defensive representative of management in a classic "me–you" confrontation, now they began more and more to address the group as a group. Prodded by closer involvement of the president, executive members grew less hesitant to help develop production employees' ideas when they felt they had merit. It was now regarded as a plus for any executive when his circle came up with a good, usable idea.

Off and Crawling

Given all this, it would appear that the program was finally off and dashing headlong toward success. Not so. It ran headlong, instead, into three new problems.

First was the problem of time. Meetings were scheduled for two hours, once a month. Management, of course, paid for this time. The committee meetings with department heads following each circle meeting varied from a half to one and a half hours, depending on the number, complexity, and touchiness of the items on the agendas. The cost in terms of money and lost production time was beginning to be felt. The rewards were nowhere near commensurate. The tail was beginning to wag the dog.

The second problem was a people one. While some progress had been made, the program still did not slide smoothly into place. There was still an unbalancing undercurrent of distrust between the ranks that flared up occasionally like sunspots, and the false start of the first attempt had in some cases hardened this distrust instead of serving as a cornerstone upon which to build the second attempt. The president found he had to spend more time than he had planned visiting circle meetings, massaging some bruised egos, and riding shotgun on some reluctant unconvinced managers.

The third problem surfaced right after the meetings began, when the president discovered that most of the circles quickly began to go sterile in the idea department. They seemingly ran out of ideas after having given voice to the more obvious ones, such as the four-day, 10-hours-a-day week and job rotation to relieve boredom. All in all, the program in practice, despite a few breakthrough achievements, was not far from being totally useless.

With grim determination, the president went back to the drawing board.

Home at Last

Coming to grips with the deficiencies of his part-time efforts, the president decided to set up a full-time circle program administrator. He selected a young, sharp, energetic, gutsy engineer from the manufacturing engineering department. To give him muscle, he was to report to the president once a week, giving him a *full* review of what had taken place during that week. He was relieved of all other duties. The president was determined not to be surprised again.

Moving quickly, the administrator eliminated from each circle both the outside executive and the committees that met with department heads following each circle meeting. Instead, he assumed their functions. Attending each circle meeting, he took the comments and suggestions that came out of them, refined them with the participants into meaningful form, and then guided them through to the appropriate levels of management. He reported back to the various circles with the results, reasons for acceptance or rejection, and implementation schedules for those accepted. This sharply reduced the total man-hours formerly expended by the committees.

Next he rescheduled the two-hour, once-a-month circle meetings to a leaner one-half to three-quarters of an hour, twice a month. At the same time, he redefined their purpose. Originally, the president had envisioned the circles as self-generating, perpetually producing factories of new ideas. They were not, of course, and never could be. With more precision, the administrator saw their purpose in terms of three goals:

1. To provide the vehicle for better cost and quality control by generating and focusing more individual awareness and participation in the achievement of both, and to provide the vehicle for introducing fresh thinking and old experience at the production floor levels to current and new evolving problems.

2. To tie all levels of management and labor to the same company goals, making their efforts mutually supportive by introducing an effective system of two-way communications.

3. To serve as a safety valve for any conflicts or tensions that might build up from time to time. To achieve these goals, he took the following steps.

As noted, he made the path of ideas from inception to final decision less cumbersome by handling himself the process of final definition, refinement, and presentation. Being an able engineer with a whole lot of smarts of the homegrown practical variety, he could present the ideas in terms that had practical relevance. When, for example, a circle came up with a presumed cost-savings idea to speed up a production line and at the same time add two people to it to ensure success, he fleshed out the idea by developing the actual cost trade-offs and possible complications before presenting it upstairs. This resulted in less time and effort slippage and involved fewer people than the previous committee method. And knowing that their ideas would be refined before being submitted for consideration, the circles became less hesitant to express more ideas in rough, unfinished form.

Once the lines of communication were functioning and management began to listen and labor felt it was beginning to be listened to, the program administrator gradually brought upstairs downstairs by encouraging more executives to actively participate in circle meetings, reducing even further the distance between the two groups. His unbridled enthusiasm, his calculated, disarming bluntness ("The president sure will be pleased to know that you dropped in on two circle meetings this week"), and his weekly reporting to the president gave him enough influence with the levels of management he had to deal with to make them more congenial to the idea of participating in the spirit of the program. Eventually, the increased level of participation reduced a good deal of the mutual distrust between the various participants.

Guiding Idea Development

To solve the problem of idea sterility and recognizing that ideas usually come about as specific responses to defined problems and opportunities, and generally don't just burst forth because a group of people are gathered around a table and told to think, the program administrator took steps to define these problems and opportunities meaningfully.

From the start, of course, the circle program revolved around a central theme of "quality and cost." On a practical basis, not only was a better made, less expensive product more salable, but it was also a source of pride (especially quality that could in many respects actually be seen, touched, and compared). The administrator, now pretty well plugged into the realities of the program, saw the effectiveness of a quality control program in terms of ensuring a *continuing* undiminished interest on the part of those making the product.

With this in mind, he continually brought the more tangible effects of both good and bad quality closer to the people who had to deal with them every day. He circulated letters of complaint (or praise) from customers at each meeting. He also expressed in dollars the costs of poor quality in terms of rejects, returns, and reworks, and conversely laid out the positive cost-effect of better quality in terms of reducing these costs. He brought salesmen in from the field to talk about their problems, to explain by specific examples the price competition they were facing, the real-world effects of late deliveries, and how only one defective shipment could screw up months of effort to sell an account against the competition. This tuned all hands, including some tunnel-visioned management people, closer to the realities of that arena of final, stark truth—the marketplace.

To further develop an effective two-way communications system, the administrator held combined circle meetings, bringing in other management people to explain how costs were derived, what *overhead* meant and how it affected the final selling price, and why profits were necessary to generate funds for reinvestment and to stimulate new investment. Marketing people were brought in to discuss their present problems, what they were doing about them, what plans they had for the future in terms of new products and new markets, and what the competition was up to. Management people were generally encouraged to talk about their jobs, what they did, how they did it, their problems in getting it done, and how what they did contributed to the total effort. These presentations were limited to a tight 15 minutes each, with a question, answer, and comment period following.

Production people, workers, foremen, and the like were called upon to present status and progress reports on new ideas and procedures that were being implemented at their levels. If, for example, a foreman reported progress in reducing rejects, the administrator saw to it that his report was seconded by a quality control engineer and that the foreman was thanked for his efforts by the executive concerned with his department.

Knowing and better understanding the real-world problems of developing, financing, producing, and selling a product, against other organizations trying to do the same thing in the same market, served to help focus the circles' efforts to make whatever contribution they could to further these ends. ("Remember this," a marketing manager noted in his addresses to the circles, "when a crunch comes, as it does from time to time, the guys who make the better product, who can sell it for less, who can sell it smarter, are the guys who keep their jobs. That's you and me." Noted the controller, "When a company falls on hard times or doesn't grow, it's very easy to blame 'them.' Just remember, in the final analysis, you and me together *are* 'them.' It's our problem and our opportunity. I sure as hell can't do it alone, and neither can you. But *we* can.")

Footnote

The 12 circles were originally composed of about 100 employees, representing a total work force of about 600. As soon as he felt everyone was comfortable with the program, and had worked into it, the administrator encouraged each circle to increase its membership to what it felt was still a manageable number, and in some cases, he helped it subdivide from one to two circles. Each circle named a coordinator, whose job it was to arrange for those not actively participating in a circle but who had ideas they wanted to discuss to attend and present their ideas. He set up a policy of membership rotation so that everyone would have an opportunity to participate.

He established a company newsletter, not to cover such breathtaking news as who had a baby in Department 14 and to congratulate Peter Pickle for completing 20 years of loyal and devoted service, but to let everybody know "just what the hell is going on." The title, "Update," is indicative of the purpose. Included are new ideas and projects (with both the circle and the people who suggested them given credit), the action taken, and, as soon as they can be measured, the results. Even some ideas that can't be implemented are reviewed, and the reasons why given. Customers' letters are printed. If the letter is a complaint, the newsletter indicates what is being done about it, or asks what can be done. Every issue reviews some activity that management is taking to hold up its end, including marketing plans and why and where new investments are being made. (One compounding machine operator suggested that the newsletter would make a great public relations vehicle to show how serious the company and its people were in ferreting out, serving, and satisfying its customers' needs. Enthusiastically, marketing prepared a customer mailing list and plans were formulated to go from copy-machine reprints to slick paper. At this writing, however, the company is having second thoughts. There is a fear that maybe "we'd be letting too many secrets out of the bag. Why provide a blueprint for our competition?")

What Happened

The successful results of these efforts did not occur all at once. Whatever good came out of the program evolved slowly. The process of evolution was laced with heartbreaks, disappointments, jealousies, false starts, misdirections, and enough initial cynicism to fill a tank car. But it did work—finally.

The improvement in product quality began to take significant root as everyone came to the realization that this time the program *was* going to work, that it *had* to work, and that a wholehearted commitment was being made to make it work. In time, virtually each employee became a quality inspector. Even many of those holding tight to their cynical distrusts finally succumbed to peer pressure. Company goals, plans, and objectives were now better understood, as were the viewpoints and attitudes of both production employees and managers.

In one of the two companies used in this case (privately owned), production costs went down 6 percent in the first 8 months, leveled off for the next 4, then increased 2 percent in the next 4 as a result of better morale, less absenteeism, a reduction in quality rejects, the number of usable ideas that emerged from the circles, and a more cooperative implementation of management policies. Adjusting for inflation, costs in terms of stable dollars declined about 9½ percent over the 16-month period. At the end of the first 12 months, production workers and most middle and lower managers received a lump-sum profit-sharing bonus equivalent to 3½ percent of their past year's pay. (One interesting sidelight: In one company where the union felt that its authority was being diluted and circumvented, management wisely let the circle council handle the problem. It did. It told the shop steward to shut up and tend his machine and told the business agent to take a hike. They'd let him know when they needed him.) In the second company, which had a stock purchase plan, employee stock purchases the first year picked up 26 percent.

If one descriptive adjective emerged from the program, it was the word *mutual*. Greater mutual respect, understanding, and support were the principle derivatives. The working atmospheres became more relaxed. Most everyone developed a recognition of the importance of everyone elses'—*and their own*—contribution to the solutions of common problems and the achievement of mutual goals. In a broad sense, work became less of a thankless chore. It now took on a more defined and rewarding purpose. Although the whole effort was far from perfect, the program worked in terms of results.

THE ROCKY ROAD

Any program to foster positive orientation and cooperation between the various levels of an organization has some tough built-in problems that must be reckoned with. One of these arises from our propensity to deal in stereotypes. Many managers have lived so long with the attitude that production employees are merely pairs of hands required to do the dirty work, they find it difficult to adjust to sharing the creative process with them. "Hell, they really don't care," snarled one manager. "They'll screw the company any chance they get. The only thing they care about is how to get more goof-off time at more money."

Often used to staff meetings where the participants can communicate comfortably with commonly understood buzz words, sometimes used to managing by memo, remote from their effects and nuances at the implementation levels, many executives harbor a subtle contempt for those who don't have a desk on which to put a tray of paper clips and pictures of the spouse and kids. To share the responsibility and credit for the success of the company with such people is, some feel, not only a waste of time but a repudiation of the successes they've achieved by years of education, hard work, effective production, diligent application, and occasional apple polishing. As one manager put it, "I made it on my own. I worked my way through school, and no one gave me a leg up. I'm here because I earned it working my butt off 10–12 hours a day. I report to enough superiors. I'll be damned if I'm going to take the time to justify any decisions I make to a guy on the production who couldn't care less. Let him do his job, and I'll do mine."

Some managers' game plan is to get experience where they are, later sell it to another company at a higher salary, and keep duplicating the process until they reach wherever their top is. Some feel they want to make a good showing where they are and either find a secure and comfortable niche where they can burrow in free from harassment or edge upward as new slots open. Frequently, their attitude is, "If somebody on the factory floor is going to stumble on a good idea that I'd have come up with eventually or if we're going to share my level of management with the labor force, somebody higher up is going to scratch his head and wonder what the hell do they need me for?"

The production worker—who is accustomed to worrying about how to pay for the new car he needs or how to handle the problem of the kid's new braces; who has faced layoffs, maybe strikes, the whole gamut of job insecurity; who is bored silly with his job; who feels that any proposal by management can only have the one purpose of squeezing more out of his gut; who will share in the benefits of productivity only when he himself can wrench it out of a reluctant management's hide—lives with the idea that only he and his co-workers are losing the race with the cost of living, while "they" (management and stockholders) not only are indifferent to the workers' plight but are more concerned with how to finagle a deduction out of a company-paid country club membership. Obviously, these stereotypical perceptions, with or without merit, impose significant barriers to the smooth implementation of a participative management program.

Another problem can best be illustrated by the cultural difference between the Japanese and American manager and worker in their orientations toward groups. The Japanese cultural experience is one of group effort, and the emphasis is on the contribution that one can make to the success of the group. To do this, the manager or worker is willing to submerge a good part of his ego to the effort. In return, his future is secured as part of the group. The American, on the other hand, is culturally highly individualistic (shades of Tom Sawyer, Horatio Alger, wagon-trains-across-the-prairie syndrome). He's on his own. No one's going to look out for him, except himself (or his union, which by definition is an adversary of management). His first loyalty is to himself and his family, and his loyalty to the group comes way down the line, if at all. He has not been made to feel that his security is tied in to the group effort as has his Japanese counterpart. And in a sense, of course, he's right.

(Oddly, where the Japanese have tried circle programs in this country, for the most part they've worked—and with good reason. The Japanese part of the management team already comes well tuned in to making it work. American workers and managers exposed to the program in a new company where there are no previous antagonisms to overcome, no unions with which to battle for position, and where the work force is generally younger and less set in its ways, seem fervently determined to make it work.)

Another problem that must be faced is managerial perspective. If a program is to be set up, it inevitably comes about through management initiative. Thus, there is a natural tendency to view it from a narrow management perspective, to assume that giving employees the opportunity to express themselves creatively will provide the motivation for their active and cooperative participation. "You talk, we'll listen" is the essence of such a program. Or in other cases, management feels that workers will feel pumped up if management takes them into its confidence in making them privy to management's problems and objectives. This approach says, "We'll talk, you listen."

Whichever way it goes, a one-way communications system

generally falls far short. Frequently (not always; again, it depends on the personality of the organization and how hard the listeners really listen) management suddenly finds that no one's talking, no one's listening, and no one's licking anyone's hand out of gratitude for this opportunity. In many cases, the program flops and management, instead of trying to give it more substance, simply decides that the whole concept is a waste of time and that its employees probably don't have much to say anyway.

Still another problem, going the other way, is that in a few cases an optimistic management, thoroughly misunderstanding the purpose and philosophy of the program, has set up circles (or committees or whatever form it takes) with the expectation that production employees will begin to manage their own activities and that management will simply provide guidance and direction. This has led to a few mob scenes reminiscent of the adventures of the Keystone Cops. The fact is management must still manage. It can delegate and share, but it is naive to think it can successfully abdicate its ultimate responsibility to manage without having, among other things, disjointed goal targeting. For a program to work, there must be competence and discipline (not necessarily the rigid variety) at every level, and that includes managerial competence and discipline. If an employee senses that he's being managed by dummies, his tendency is to view the whole process with contempt. Delegating and sharing is a vital part of a successful program. Abdication of responsibility is not.

Time is another pothole on the rocky road to setting up a program. Programs take time—time to organize, to set up, to administer, to operate, to adjust and fine tune, to handle problems, to investigate and develop ideas and new approaches, to implement those that are implementable, and to communicate. Any participative management program is going to take time, and if an organization stumbles into it expecting that somehow its structure and administration will seek its own level and take shape by itself, the time factor can become excessive and crippling. If the thrust of the program is that it is an end unto itself rather than a means to an end (this end being clear-cut goals and objectives), the time consumed will almost inevitably outweigh any results.

WHAT'S NEEDED—A SUMMARY

Given all these problems, a close, cooperative, mutually supportive involvement of the various levels of an organization—this ultimate in positive orientation—requires:

1. A total management commitment. "Let's try this and see what happens" is not the same as "We're going to set up a program. It's going to work because we're going to make it work. And it's going to pay off." It needs someone with enough muscle and smarts to administer it, bridge the various levels, and connect the varying concerns.

2. In the organizational stage, all levels that will participate should be consulted, informed of the purpose and goals, and asked for advice on setting up the most appropriate procedures for making it work. The purpose of the program should be clearly defined. It can be survival or growth or job security in the face of toughening competition or changing business climates.

3. A reward system should, of course, be built into the program—profit sharing, or stock purchase opportunities, or a pat on the back, or recognition, more job growth opportunities, relief from boredom, opportunities for pride of contribution.

4. The structure should be fluid enough to change as needed, to rebuild from failures and to build on successes, to adapt to the changing pecularities and needs of the organization. Management's commitment must be consistent, constant, and realistic.

5. And, above all, the communications process:

$$listen \leftrightarrow explain \leftrightarrow listen$$

must go two ways, up and down. Patronization, insincerity, cynicism, especially on the part of management, should be avoided like seven and a half plagues. The program is essentially a people program, and people will react negatively to negative stimuli and positively to positive stimuli.

Participation means positive involvement. Positive involvement is rooted in knowing what's going on and what it's going to take to make certain things happen. Motivation is rooted in knowing *why* certain things should happen and "what's in it for me?" if those things do happen. This takes communication, and communication is rooted in *listening* and explaining. Put it all together, and you've got positive orientation.

INDEX

AMACOM Paperbacks

John Fenton	The A To Z Of Sales Management	$ 7.95	07580
Hank Seiden	Advertising Pure And Simple	$ 7.95	07510
Alice G. Sargent	The Androgynous Manager	$ 8.95	07601
John D. Arnold	The Art Of Decision Making	$ 6.95	07537
Oxenfeldt & Miller & Dickinson	A Basic Approach To Executive Decision Making	$ 7.95	07551
Curtis W. Symonds	Basic Financial Management	$ 7.95	07563
William R. Osgood	Basics Of Successful Business Planning	$ 7.95	07579
Dickens & Dickens	The Black Manager	$10.95	07564
Ken Cooper	Bodybusiness	$ 5.95	07545
Jones & Trentin	Budgeting	$12.95	07528
Laura Brill	Business Writing Quick And Easy	$ 5.95	07598
Rinella & Robbins	Career Power	$ 7.95	07586
Andrew H. Souerwine	Career Strategies	$ 7.95	07535
Beverly A. Potter	Changing Performance On The Job	$ 9.95	07613
Donna N. Douglass	Choice And Compromise	$ 8.95	07604
Philip R. Lund	Compelling Selling	$ 8.95	07506
Joseph M. Vles	Computer Basics	$ 6.95	07599
Hart & Schleicher	A Conference And Workshop Planner's Manual	$15.95	07003
Leon Wortman	A Deskbook Of Business Management	$14.95	07571
John D. Drake	Effective Interviewing	$ 8.95	07600
James J. Cribbin	Effective Managerial Leadership	$ 6.95	07504
Eugene J. Benge	Elements Of Modern Management	$ 5.95	07519
James E. Kristy & Susan Z. Diamond	Finance Without Fear	$10.95	07587
Edward N. Rausch	Financial Management For Small Business	$ 7.95	07585
Loren B. Belker	The First-Time Manager	$ 6.95	07588
Whitsett & Yorks	From Management Theory to Business Sense	$17.95	07610
Ronald D. Brown	From Selling To Managing	$ 7.95	07500
Murray L. Weidenbaum	The Future Of Business Regulation	$ 5.95	07533
Craig S. Rice	Getting Good People And Keeping Them	$ 8.95	07614
Charles Hughes	Goal Setting	$ 4.95	07520
Richard E. Byrd	A Guide To Personal Risk Taking	$ 7.95	07505
Charles Margerison	How To Assess Your Managerial Style	$ 6.95	07584
S.H. Simmons	How To Be The Life Of The Podium	$ 8.95	07565
D. German & J. German	How To Find A Job When Jobs Are Hard To Find	$ 7.95	07592

W.H. Krause	How To Get Started As A Manufacturer's Representative	$ 8.95	07574
Sal T. Massimino	The Complete Book of Closing Sales	$ 5.95	07593
William A. Delaney	How To Run A Growing Company	$ 6.95	07590
Dean B. Peskin	A Job Loss Survival Manual	$ 5.95	07543
H. Lee Rust	Jobsearch	$ 7.95	07557
Marc J. Lane	Legal Handbook For Small Business	$ 7.95	07612
George T. Vardaman	Making Successful Presentations	$10.95	07616
Norman L. Enger	Management Standards For Developing Information Systems	$ 5.95	07527
Ray A. Killian	Managing Human Resources	$ 6.95	07556
Elam & Paley	Marketing For The Non-Marketing Executive	$ 5.95	07562
Edward S. McKay	The Marketing Mystique	$ 6.95	07522
Donald E. Miller	The Meaningful Interpretation Of Financial Statements	$ 6.95	07513
Robert L. Montgomery	Memory Made Easy	$ 5.95	07548
Donald P. Kenney	Minicomputers	$ 7.95	07560
Frederick D. Buggie	New Product Development Strategies	$ 8.95	07602
Dale D. McConkey	No-Nonsense Delegation	$ 4.95	07517
Hilton & Knoblauch	On Television	$ 6.95	07581
Ellis & Pekar	Planning Basics For Managers	$ 6.95	07591
Alfred R. Oxenfeldt	Pricing Strategies	$10.95	07572
Blake & Mouton	Productivity: The Human Side	$ 5.95	07583
Daniels & Barron	The Professional Secretary	$ 7.95	07576
Herman R. Holtz	Profit From Your Money-Making Ideas	$ 8.95	07553
William E. Rothschild	Putting It All Together	$ 7.95	07555
J.F. Engelberger	Robotics In Practice	$24.95	07587
Don Sheehan	Shut Up And Sell!	$ 7.95	07615
Roger W. Seng	The Skills Of Selling	$ 7.95	07547
Hannan & Berrian & Cribbin & Donis	Success Strategies For The New Sales Manager	$ 8.95	07566
Paula I. Robbins	Successful Midlife Career Change	$ 7.95	07536
Leon Wortman	Successful Small Business Management	$ 8.95	07503
D. Bennett	TA And The Manager	$ 4.95	07511
George A. Brakeley, Jr.	Tested Ways To Successful Fund-Raising	$ 8.95	07568
William A. Delaney	Tricks Of The Manager's Trade	$ 6.95	07603
Alec Benn	The 27 Most Common Mistakes In Advertising	$ 8.95	07554
James Gray, Jr.	The Winning Image	$ 6.95	07611
John Applegath	Working Free	$ 6.95	07582
Allen Weiss	Write What You Mean	$ 5.95	07544
Richard J. Dunsing	You And I Have Simply Got To Stop Meeting This Way	$ 5.95	07558